How to Open & Operate a Financially Successful
MEDICAL BILLING SERVICE:
With Companion CD-ROM

by Laura Louise Gater

HOW TO OPEN & OPERATE A FINANCIALLY SUCCESSFUL MEDICAL BILLING SERVICE: WITH COMPANION CD-ROM

Copyright © 2010 Atlantic Publishing Group, Inc.
1405 SW 6th Avenue • Ocala, Florida 34471 • Phone 800-814-1132 • Fax 352-622-1875
Web site: www.atlantic-pub.com • E-mail: sales@atlantic-pub.com
SAN Number: 268-1250

Library of Congress Cataloging-in-Publication Data

Gater, Laura.
  How to open and operate a financially successful medical billing service : with companion CD-ROM / by Laura Gater.
     p. cm.
  Includes bibliographical references and index.
  ISBN-13: 978-1-60138-280-1 (alk. paper)
  ISBN-10: 1-60138-280-4 (alk. paper)
  1. Medical economics. I. Title.
  R728.G27 2010
  338.4'73621--dc22
                          2009054256

Printed in the United States

PROJECT MANAGER: Amy Moczynski • amoczynski@atlantic-pub.com
PEER REVIEWER: Marilee Griffin • mgriffin@atlantic-pub.com
INTERIOR DESIGN: James Ryan Hamilton • www.jamesryanhamilton.com
ASSISTANT EDITOR: Angela Pham • apham@atlantic-pub.com
FRONT & BACK COVER DESIGN: Jackie Miller • millerjackiej@gmail.com

Printed on Recycled Paper

We recently lost our beloved pet "Bear," who was not only our best and dearest friend but also the "Vice President of Sunshine" here at Atlantic Publishing. He did not receive a salary but worked tirelessly 24 hours a day to please his parents. Bear was a rescue dog that turned around and showered myself, my wife, Sherri, his grandparents Jean, Bob, and Nancy, and every person and animal he met (maybe not rabbits) with friendship and love. He made a lot of people smile every day.

We wanted you to know that a portion of the profits of this book will be donated to The Humane Society of the United States. —*Douglas & Sherri Brown*

The human-animal bond is as old as human history. We cherish our animal companions for their unconditional affection and acceptance. We feel a thrill when we glimpse wild creatures in their natural habitat or in our own backyard.

Unfortunately, the human-animal bond has at times been weakened. Humans have exploited some animal species to the point of extinction.

The Humane Society of the United States makes a difference in the lives of animals here at home and worldwide. The HSUS is dedicated to creating a world where our relationship with animals is guided by compassion. We seek a truly humane society in which animals are respected for their intrinsic value, and where the human-animal bond is strong.

Want to help animals? We have plenty of suggestions. Adopt a pet from a local shelter, join The Humane Society and be a part of our work to help companion animals and wildlife. You will be funding our educational, legislative, investigative and outreach projects in the U.S. and across the globe.

Or perhaps you'd like to make a memorial donation in honor of a pet, friend or relative? You can through our Kindred Spirits program. And if you'd like to contribute in a more structured way, our Planned Giving Office has suggestions about estate planning, annuities, and even gifts of stock that avoid capital gains taxes.

Maybe you have land that you would like to preserve as a lasting habitat for wildlife. Our Wildlife Land Trust can help you. Perhaps the land you want to share is a backyard—that's enough. Our Urban Wildlife Sanctuary Program will show you how to create a habitat for your wild neighbors.

So you see, it's easy to help animals. And The HSUS is here to help.

2100 L Street NW • Washington, DC 20037 • 202-452-1100
www.hsus.org

Dedication

I dedicate this book to my loving husband, Steve, who has always been supportive of my freelance writing career and anything else that I do.

Trademark Disclaimer

All trademarks, trade names, or logos mentioned or used are the property of their respective owners and are used only to directly describe the products being provided. Every effort has been made to properly capitalize, punctuate, identify, and attribute trademarks and trade names to their respective owners, including the use of ® and ™ wherever possible and practical. Atlantic Publishing Group, Inc. is not a partner, affiliate, or licensee with the holders of said trademarks.

Contents

Chapter 4: Software Choices   65

Chapter 5: Starting Your Medical Billing Business   83

Chapter 6: Establishing a Business Plan   107

Chapter 7: Financing Your New Business   123

Chapter 8: New Business Basics   139

Introduction

The health care industry provides more than 14 million jobs, and it is estimated that the industry will generate 3.2 million more jobs between 2008 and 2018 — more than any other industry, according to the Bureau of Labor Statistics (**www.bls.gov/oco/cg/cgs035.htm**). If you are detailed-oriented, want to be your own boss, and would like to act on the behalf of physicians all over the country, the medical billing service business could be the right fit for you. If you have the desire, the commitment, and the patience, then you are reading the right book. The medical billing business is thriving and expanding every day. There are many opportunities and a great deal of competition.

According to the American Medical Association (AMA), the average number of medical claims each physician generates per month is 440. Someone has to process each physician's 440 medical claims, and it might as well be you.

What is Medical Billing?

Medical billing is the procedure of obtaining payment for services health care providers give to a patient. Most people have some type of health insurance that will pay for at least part of their medical bills. The patient's medical bill (claim) must be given to the insurance company for payment. Most claims today are submitted electronically; in this case, all of the information required must be submitted in a specific format that the insurance company requires. Once a claim is received, it will be denied, paid, or held for further information.

To complicate matters, some people have more than one health care insurance policy. They may have a policy through their job, and their spouse may also have one that covers the entire family instead of just an individual. In such cases, the primary carrier, or insurance company, must be billed first, and then the balance is billed to the secondary carrier, along with the primary insurance company information.

Medical insurance billers (MIBs) usually obtain an associate's degree from a junior or community college. *Degrees and certifications are discussed in Chapter 1.*

According to the U.S. Bureau of Labor Statistics (BLS), the need for medical records and health information technicians is anticipated to grow by 20 percent through 2018 — surpassing the average for all professions. As of May 2008, health information and medical records technicians earned on average $32,960 per year. The lowest 10 percent made an annual salary of around $20,440, and the highest 10 percent earned an annual paycheck of more than $50,060, according to the BLS. Salary ranges vary according to geographic area as well as to the type of employer (hospital, private practice, outpatient care center, or long-term care or rehab center). Most MIBs work regular daytime hours, but in hospitals where health information departments are often open 24 hours, MIBs may work evening or night shifts.

Another important person in the medical billing industry is a medical coder. A medical coder (which is different than a medical biller) reviews each patient's medical record to abstract and codify the services provided by the physician, ensuring that correct codes are submitted to insurance companies and that claims can be efficiently processed. Coding drives the entire medical billing process. MIBs receive codes from their clients and enter them into practice management software to submit medical claims to insurance companies and post payments from them. Billing and coding are two separate jobs and two separate functions in a health care provider's office.

Medical billing and coding are very tricky areas to master, so it is no wonder that some doctors have as many as four employees to code their services. Multiply this number by the number of doctors in the United States and it totals a lot of money that goes toward making sure that billing and coding are adequately performed.

Every insurance company interprets codes differently, so it is the medical coder's job to choose the code that best describes each medical service performed by the physician on the patient. Patients come in daily with ailments and symptoms that are hard to code, such as weak-feeling arms. Dr. Robert Lamberts from Augusta, Georgia, who is known for his blog, "Musings of a Distractable Mind," points out that there is a code for an injury involving spacecraft, but none for weak arms.

Schools, conferences, and seminars all teach medical coding to help MIBs master the ins and outs of the trade, so to speak. In 2016, the BLS expects there to be 200,000 medical coders in the United States.

Opening and maintaining any business, not just a medical billing company, is a challenge; although it may seem lonely at times, you are not alone. There are hundreds of thousands of small business owners out there and a wealth of information at your fingertips. You will find peers and mentors by searching; you will have numerous resources for support, both online and through your local business community. The business community thrives when all of its members succeed and through a commitment of time and effort, you will develop a strong network of fellow entrepreneurs through organizations such as your city's chamber of commerce. This book will help you to navigate the world of medical billing and small business; it will provide you with the tools and knowledge to create a successful enterprise.

If you cannot figure out yet what to do with your life, or you change your job every two months, then medical billing may not be for you. Starting a medical billing service is time-consuming, and you must be fully committed. Look at your organizational skills. Are they good? Are you one of those people who has a hard time keeping up with appointments or keeping track of paperwork? If so, you may want to reconsider; medical billing is an organized business and has no room for sloppiness. You must keep track of important documents, keep patients' information confidential, and stay on top of things. Everything must be neat and organized. You will have a full workload every day. Everything must be filed, and you must be on time for appointments you will schedule. You do not need a medical background to be a medical billing professional; however, having a background in medicine or medical terminology would help. There are many basic medical training courses available at your local college or even online. The most important reason today's successful medical billing professionals have thrived is because they worked hard. You will constantly be busy looking for new clients, new ideas, and new ways to advertise your business.

Owning your own medical billing business will always have drawbacks, such as the stress of having to take care of everything from finding clients, doing accounting, struggling to get claims paid, and handling any problems on your own that may arise. You must have a strict level of discipline; there is no one to tell you what you are doing wrong, and there is no one to tell you what you are doing right, either. Some people need validation at times when they are working hard. There are no coworkers to empathize with if you have a particularly challenging day. If you need help, you must seek it from others in the field and research it on your own using the Internet, books, or peers in the medical billing business. Just as you have the final say in all decisions, including the bad ones, you are responsible for all pitfalls, mistakes, challenges, and rewards that your medical billing business will encounter.

Once you have decided to become a medical billing professional, make sure you commit your time and energy to your business. You should enjoy what you do — because if you do not, you will be miserable. If you work every day at something you do not enjoy, then you will have no drive to succeed, and you will have no interest in continuing business. Many people in the medical billing field would recommend working for a medical billing company for a while to see if you truly like the work. This will also help you realize what this type of job involves on a daily basis. While working for a medical billing company, you will see what the company goes through and some of the problems that arise. You will learn right away if you think you like this job, or if you should consider other options for a home-based business.

In order to be successful as an owner and operator of a medical billing service, you need to be efficient, self-directed, and innovative. You should also have the people and sales skills necessary to effectively market your services. If you love to sell, you will have what it takes to sell your services to the medical world. It takes a lot of drive and determination, but the rewards of owning your own business and being a part of the health care community are worth the effort.

This book will take you step by step through the process of opening your own medical billing business and overcoming challenges that may arise. It includes information on home-based or office locations, equipment to purchase, and insurance. You will receive guidance on choosing the best medical billing software and a comprehensive description of medical billing services, including CPT codes, insurance carriers, guidelines, and claim preparation. You will also learn how to write a business plan, secure financing for your business, and file for appropriate licenses for your business structure. This book includes helpful information from experts who have opened their own medical billing business, including advice on how to stop claims rejection, land your first client, generate maximum income, and avoid common pitfalls. You will learn all the best marketing strategies to ensure business success, including networking and Internet advertising. This book will help you recruit and manage staff, fire employees, interact effectively with medical providers (your clients), and handle the challenges of owning a business in a service industry.

Readers will find all terms and abbreviations used in this book in the glossary at the back of the book for easier reference. In addition, sample medical insurance billing forms and templates can be found on the CD-ROM to simplify and streamline your business. This book will provide start-up information, advise you on how to pick a business name, show you how to form your medical billing business, and will help you decide if you want to be in a partnership or on your own. You will need to decide if you want to become a Limited Liability Company (LLC), corporation, or a sole proprietor. Many decisions need to be made, and plenty of research is needed to get your business started on the right foot. Starting a new business is exciting and overwhelming, and this book will help you avoid becoming confused, tense, and lost. Get ready to make your dreams and career goals come true.

Chapter 1

Industry Basics and Insurance Industry Overview

Before you do process any claims, approach any potential clients, or even think of renting office space, you must first familiarize yourself with the medical billing industry and how it works. One of the most important, if not the most important, aspects of the medical billing business is patient information. Because you are essentially transmitting a record of what happened in each patient's doctor visit to insurance companies, you must know what exactly you are sending to these payers, as well as the rules that accompany this action.

Working With Patient Information

When working with patients and doctors, you must respect privacy laws regarding medical records. Federal and state privacy laws protect both patients and doctors in this way. Everything you read about a patient on his or her medical records or on the billing information that you have needs to be kept confidential because you can be held legally responsible for any breach of medical information. It is your responsibility as an MIB to maintain patient confidentiality. One of the most important pieces of legislation enacted to maintain patient privacy is the Health Information Privacy and Accountability Act of 1996, also known as HIPAA.

HIPAA

This act guarantees federal protection for personal medical records. The true burden of the law actually falls on hospitals, physicians, and other medical organizations rather than medical insurance billing services. All health care providers that maintain, transmit, or store patient health care information are required to comply with HIPAA. Compliance can be as simple as providing authorized employees with passwords to access private patient medical records through the course of their medical billing work. You should provide a HIPAA contract (also known as a business partner agreement), which is a contract that notes your agreement that the medical records will be used only as stated in your business contract with them or by law, for all clients. You must make sure to comply with the policy by keeping all confidential paperwork, computer files, and records private. Violating HIPAA policies can be punished by ten years in prison and a $250,000 fine. Do not release any personal client information to anyone who calls and asks for it unless they can provide a release form from the doctor, hospital, or client releasing this information. Even then, verify that this information is correct (name, social security number, and so on) before providing the information to the person who has requested it. If this request for information is fraudulent or done without the patient's permission, then you will be held liable for releasing the information, and your clients will drop your services when they find out what happened. Your faxes should contain a cover statement stating the enclosed information is confidential and protected by HIPAA.

The American Health Information Management Association (AHIMA) provides a sample contractual agreement titled the "HIPAA Business Associate Agreement" that is signed by the client and your medical billing service to ensure both will follow the laws regarding patient confidentiality and health information privacy. The American Medical Association (AMA) recommends the HIPAA Authorization Form for use or disclosure of information for purposes requested by physician's office.

Besides the law, the physicians or hospitals to which you will be providing services will expect you and your employees to respect their patients' confidentiality. Do not expect to continue in business if you cannot respect your clients' right to privacy, especially with something as important as their patients' medical records. You will not last long in this business if you cannot ensure confidentiality for your clients and their patients.

After you ensure you are familiar and compliant with all HIPAA standards, you must know about different kinds of health services your clients' patients may receive. Being familiar with the different services and health coverage options will give you greater insight into the billing industry.

Categories of Health Services

There are many health services that insurance companies will cover, such as medical, psychiatric, dental, durable medical equipment, and pharmacy coverage options. Your medical care normally consists of testing for illnesses, hospital stays, preventative care, emergency room visits, and prescription drugs. There are other kinds of services that are not covered under a regular medical insurance plan, including dental care, vision coverage, and mental health care. Some patients may choose services depending on what they need the help with most. If they only go to the doctor for a vision screening once a year or not at all, they may feel it is not necessary to purchase vision coverage, while someone else may think purchasing vision insurance is necessary because they go to the doctor often.

Below are the different kinds of services you may bill for, depending on what type of practice your clients run.

Medical services

Medical services are those related to a person's physical health. They can include immunizations, a blood test or X-ray, or follow-up care for a chronic medical illness. Medical services may be performed:

- In a doctor's office

- In a walk-in clinic

- In an emergency care clinic

- In a hospital emergency room (hospital outpatient)

- In an ambulance

- At the site of an accident or injury (by emergency medical technicians, or EMTs)

- In a hospital (inpatient)

- In a nursing home or long-term care center

- In a retail business (such as CVS or Walgreens)

- At an industry or job site health care center

- By an off-site service provider

Psychiatric services

These types of services help people with mental and emotional issues, such as problems with their families or depression, and they also are often used for help with drug and alcohol abuse. Psychologists, psychiatrists, counselors, and social workers all provide psychiatric services to benefit their clients' mental and emotional health. Psychiatric services include counseling, group therapy, marital therapy, mediation between family members, and more. Those who provide psychiatric services can determine which type of service is most beneficial for their clients based on their needs. Many insurance carriers provide coverage for certain types of psychiatric services and treatment.

Dental services

Dental services are provided by dentists, orthodontists, and other oral health specialists. These types of doctors provide any care related to the teeth and mouth. If there is more of a problem, dentists will refer patients to a doctor who specializes in particular types of teeth and mouth injuries or diseases. A dentist provides preventive tooth care (such as cleaning teeth and giving fluoride treatment to prevent cavities) while orthodontists provide braces to correct tooth and mouth irregularities. Oral surgeons extract teeth and provide other types of dental surgery. A periodontist prevents, diagnoses, and treats diseases of the teeth and surrounding tissue, while an endodontist diagnoses, prevents, and treats diseases and injuries of dental pulp and dental roots. Many of these dental services are reimbursed if a patient has dental insurance coverage.

Durable medical equipment

Durable medical equipment refers to equipment that is needed in and around the home for medical services needs. Some examples are walkers, lift chairs, hospital beds, elevated toilet seats, and oxygen tanks and tubing. Some durable medical equipment may be provided by a physician, hospital, or home health agency, but others can be purchased as needed by a patient or family member. Physicians and therapists usually need to obtain authorization from the payer (insurance company, Medicare, or Medicaid) before rental or purchase of supplies, equipment, orthotics, and prosthetics. The payer often has the right to select the vendors from which these items must be rented or purchased. All medical supplies and durable medical equipment require a prescription from a physician. If the physician has a "supplies and medical equipment" category of service, he or she may be reimbursed for medical supplies or durable medical equipment dispensed for use in the patient's home. Physicians must have a valid Medicaid Provider Agreement in order to be eligible to apply for and receive a supplies and medical equipment category of service.

Pharmacy services

Pharmacy services occur when patients go to a pharmacy and fill prescriptions from their doctors. Many hospitals, nursing homes, and even medical office complexes also have pharmacies where people can have their prescriptions filled and maybe buy some durable medical equipment or other items they need related to health care.

Insurance Options

After you become comfortable with the different types of service patients may receive, you must learn about the different kinds of insurance. Below is a list of common health insurance terms and their definitions:

- **Carrier:** Also known as the administrator, insurer, payer, and underwriter; writes and administrates the insurance policies.

- **Government policies:** Medicare and Medicaid programs. *More about these plans is explained later in this chapter.*

- **Individual policies:** These types of policies are medical insurance coverage for a single person or family.

- **Group policies:** These policies are for employers to purchase for their employees.

- **Provider:** This is anyone who provides any type of medical care and treatment.

- **Dependents:** Person directly related to, or dependent upon, the insured (normally refers to spouse and/or children).

- **Insured:** Person who owns and is covered by an insurance policy.

- **Beneficiary:** Anyone who receives benefits from any type of insurance policy.

- **Deductible:** The amount a patient must pay before his or her insurance company will cover any medical costs. After the deductible is paid, the patient's insurance will pay the rest of the bill. If the patient is in the hospital and his or her insurance deductible is $300, and the bill comes to a total of $1,200, the patient must then pay the $300 deductible first; then, the insurance company will pay the remaining amount, which in this case would be $900.

Many states have their own insurance plans, such as Florida KidCare, a program that offers health insurance for all children in the state until they are 18 years old. Aside from the various state-wide health insurance plans, there are several plans that offer national coverage. There are two kinds of national insurance this chapter will cover: government-run plans and commercial or private insurance plans.

Government-run insurance

TRICARE

This insurance is available to all members of the armed services, their families, and survivors. TRICARE is also offered to retired military personnel and offers pharmacy coverage, dental plans, and TRICARE for Life, which provides health coverage to TRICARE beneficiaries who are older than age 65.

Workers' compensation

The Office of Workers' Compensation Programs, which is run under the U.S. Department of Labor, administers the workers' compensation program. This insurance coverage ensures anyone who is injured on the job is able to receive wage replacement benefits, medical treatment, vocational rehabilitation, and other benefits to anyone who becomes injured while working (such as coal miners who experience black lung disease). This insurance also covers dependents who may suffer work-related injuries or occupational diseases.

Medicaid

Medicaid is a government health insurance program for low-income individuals who are unable to afford health care coverage, and also for those who are disabled and cannot pay for medical insurance. Medicaid claims are processed by private insurance carriers, which vary by state. Medicaid fees are subject to constant changes, and an MIB must keep up with all of the latest rules and regulations regarding them. These rules and regulations are published in the Third-Party Payer Directory. This publication provides detailed information about medical claims processing, instructions for how to complete claims processing forms, and a listing of more than 2,000 third-party payers and regulatory agencies.

Medicare

Medicare is a federal health insurance program for retirees age 65 or over, for those who are blind and/or disabled of any age, and for those who have End Stage Renal Disease (ESRD). Those who are covered on Medicare are not able to apply for coverage for Medicaid as well. Medicare has two parts, Part A and Part B. Part A pays for skilled nursing facilities, hospitalization, home health care, and hospice care but does not include long-term or custodial care. Part B pays for medically necessary inpatient or outpatient doctor care and some services Part A does not cover, including occupations therapies and home health care services. Part B will also cover preventative services.

Your medical billing business can get free software from Medicare for electronic transmissions. Medicare pays only 80 percent of the bill, and then the rest is up to the patient or a secondary insurance provider. Medicare fees and coverage are subject to frequent changes, and a MIB must keep up with all of the latest rules and regulations regarding them, with the help of the Third Party Payer Directory and notices from the Centers for Medicare and Medicaid Services (CMS).

Medigap

Medigap is Medicare Supplement Insurance, which helps Medicare recipients pay the difference between the health care costs covered by Medicare and what they owe. Medigap is health insurance sold by private insurance companies. Medigap "fills in the gaps" left in Medicare — for co-insurance, non-covered services, and deductibles. Someone who buys Medigap must have Medicare Part A and Medicare Part B. You, the MIB, will process the claim by putting the patient's Medigap policy number on the Medicare claim and sending the claim on to Medicare. Medicare will process the claim and then automatically forward it to the Medigap insurance carrier.

Commercial/private insurance carriers

This group represents national, private insurance plans, such as UnitedHealthcare® or Wellpoint®, that are often provided through employers. There are three different types of insurance in the commercial, or private, health insurance business:

- **Basic plan**: This type of insurance plan covers only a certain aspect of health care or services, such as hospital visits only. Basic plans are usually very inexpensive, with no deductible or a low deductible. They have a low maximum amount payable, such as $5,000 (amounts vary by provider or insurance company). Most basic plans do not cover cosmetic surgery and mental disorders.

- **Major medical plan**: Major medical plans are generally designed to cover catastrophic medical situations, such as extended hospitalization, and usually do not cover office visits, minor health problems, or prescriptions. Major medical plans commonly have large co-payments and large deductibles.

- **Comprehensive medical plan**: Highest level of medical insurance coverage; a combination of the basic and the major medical plans.

Health maintenance organization (HMO)

HMOs are managed care providers who receive a monthly fee for each person in their care, regardless of whether they actually see the patient. Patients pay a low co-payment fee per visit, such as $10, and they are assigned to a particular physician. The doctor must refer a patient to a specialist if they deem it necessary; it is not permissible to go to any specialist any time the patient chooses. Medical care by any physician outside the HMO network is not covered; patients will be responsible for paying a large co-insurance fee or may not be reimbursed at all.

Managed service organization (MSO)

An MSO is a type of managed care arrangement formed by hospitals that want doctors to use their hospital for lab work, X-rays, and other services, but want the doctors to see patients in the doctors' offices.

Exclusive provider organization (EPO)

An EPO is almost like an HMO. Patients can only see doctors inside their network, and the network is selected by the insurer. If patients see a doctor outside the network, they are responsible for the entire cost. Reimbursement to providers is based on predetermined fee-for-service rates.

Independent practice association (IPA)

An IPA results when an HMO contracts with independent physicians or associations to care for its members. Some IPAs result from physicians organizing their own association and asking HMOs for contracts. Physicians may care for their non-HMO patients on a fee-for-service basis. Some IPAs are prepaid plans on a capitation basis, which is a method of paying for health care based on the number of patients who are covered for a specific period of time rather than the number of services provided.

Preferred provider organization (PPO)

A PPO is similar to an HMO in that it consists of a network of physicians. Patients have more choice as to their medical care providers and pay a lower co-pay by going to a care provider in their PPO. A PPO does not assign doctors to certain patients. A PPO is more expensive than an HMO. If PPO patients see a physician outside the PPO network, then they pay a higher co-insurance rate or sometimes they are responsible for the entire fee.

Point of service plan (POS)

A POS Plan is where patients must see an assigned primary care physician in their provider network, thus these plans are often called a hybrid PPO/HMO plan. Members are responsible for payment for visits to providers outside the POS.

Insurance Verification

Make sure your clients (in this case, doctors' offices) ask all their patients for insurance identification cards to verify coverage for each visit. Medical offices should make a copy of the card and verify the member's insurance policy identification number or the group identification number. Your clients also need to ask Medicaid patients for proof of eligibility on every doctor's visit to be sure they are still enrolled. Often, Medicaid benefits will not be paid without proof of eligibility at every doctor's visit.

Directory of insurance carriers

When a patient claim is submitted to you (the MIB) with missing information, the *Third Party Payer Directory*, formerly known as the *Health Insurance Carrier Directory*, comes in handy. Normally when the patient visits the doctor, the patient hands his or her insurance card to the receptionist, who makes a copy of it. The insurance card provides all the information about the patient, the name of the insurance provider, and type of insurance. If you are not able to get contact information about the health insurance provider, this national directory can provide you with addresses, phone numbers, fax numbers, and Web site addresses.

Medical Ethics and Laws

Medical ethics refers to the principles of conduct of the medical profession. Practicing good ethics is, or should be, standard procedure in the medical field; it means doing what is right, regardless of the outcome. The field of medicine, even medical billing, involves helping others; therefore, the ethical standards of those in a helping profession like medicine should be high.

One of the biggest legal concerns facing the medical billing industry deals with malpractice. Malpractice, as it applies to the MIB industry, usually involves filing medical claims that have been deliberately miscoded in order to collect more money from an insurance company; incidents that involve lack of security for patient records are most likely HIPAA violations, not malpractice. A lawyer would know the fine points of the law and be able to determine the best course of action, whether it is indeed malpractice, or if the matter is related to HIPAA. The MIB must carry malpractice insurance in order to protect his or her business in this event, and the MIB must do his or her best to avoid a situation that would jeopardize his or her business. No one wants to do business with a firm that has been accused of malpractice in the medical insurance billing industry.

Getting Started in the Medical Industry

Thousands of people go to the doctor every day. Pregnant women get routine checkups from their family doctor or obstetrician throughout their pregnancy. After the baby is born, new mothers visit the pediatrician to ensure their babies are growing and gaining weight. Injured workers visit the local hospital's occupational health services to be released to go back to work. Many people change the way they look by getting tummy tucks, face-lifts, or Botox® injections. Although insurance does not cover most of these cosmetic surgeries because they are elective (not medically necessary), some are necessary and are covered by insurance; for example, a car accident victim who needs his or her face reconstructed. Health-conscious individuals visit the doctor for mammograms, prostate checks, cancer screenings, blood pressure checks, cholesterol tests, and take their babies for well-child visits. Many people visit their dentist once or twice a year to get their teeth cleaned. Health is not limited to the physical body; individuals also need health care for their minds, and often visits to psychiatrists, psychologists, and behavioral counselors can be billed to insurance companies.

There are many different medical specialties, and physicians are an integral part of these specialties. Doctors will always have medical claims that need to be filed for payment, meaning medical billers will always be a vital part of the health care system. Yet, doctors' offices today are often overwhelmed with patient care needs and cannot handle the burden of medical insurance billing, which requires a lot of knowledge and attention. Most offices do not have properly trained staff who are dedicated to medical billing, and most offices do not want to bother with billing if they can outsource it — which is where you come in to meet that need.

Medical billing is too time-consuming for doctors to perform themselves, and the reality is many people have no idea what it involves. They do not know anything about insurance reimbursement regulations, managed care, coding, and claims processing. Even though many physician's office employees are familiar with a computer, not all of them are comfortable using one, nor are they able to use medical practice management software. The diagnostic codes used in medical billing also change frequently, and most medical offices cannot spare someone to keep on top of these changes along with working with patients and handling other office duties. Your medical billing services can help an overworked doctor's office, or many overworked doctors' offices, by reducing their workload and helping ensure payment of medical insurance claims.

The baby boomers (a term often used for Americans born between 1946 and 1964), a huge segment of our population, are aging. According to the U.S. Census Bureau, there are more than 78 million baby boomers, and every hour, 330 of them turn 60 — moving them one step closer to retirement and all the changes and illnesses that those years seem to bring. The huge, rapidly aging baby boomer population means more medical bills, thus more need for MIBs to process the claims and transmit them to insurance companies to ensure doctors and hospitals get paid for their services.

In today's health care industry, a medical provider must be paid for the services they provide to be successful. Doctors would have a hard time getting paid without medical billers who submit claims for services doctors provided to patients. Submitting claims is a daunting, time-consuming, and specialized task that doctors do not have time to do themselves. It is almost impossible for the average doctor to stay on top of the number of growing insurance companies, each with its own particular guidelines, in addition to providing care to patients. Medical billing specialists handle the administrative and accounting requirements needed to help the provider earn his or her living. Americans spent more than $2 trillion on health care in 2006, and that amount is expected to double by 2017.

Not long ago, patients had to submit their own insurance claims, but this is not the case today. Today, electronic filing has many incentives, but the best ones are that physicians get paid sooner (often within 14 days), and there are fewer errors. Electronic filing users utilize a form called a day sheet, which is a form that doctors fill out after they have seen and treated each patient. Once they determine a diagnosis and a treatment plan, the doctors will check the appropriate box or boxes for the services the doctor provided to the patient during the office visit. Each box has a code, letting the MIB know what to bill for. The MIB then files a CMS 1500, the form on which all medical insurance claims must be sent, and submits the claim electronically to the insurance company.

It may sound easy, but the actual process is more involved and time-consuming when errors and rejected claims enter the picture. This book will help you learn how to deal with all the common obstacles involved in medical billing. Although a medical billing service is a good business with high earning potential, it will not be easy. Health care providers use a series of common codes for procedures, called Current Procedural Terminology (CPT) codes. The codes are published by the AMA and are updated annually. The 7,800 CPT codes each consist of five digits. Each code describes medical, surgical, laboratory, radiology, anesthesiology, and evaluation and management services of health care providers, hospitals, pharmacists, psychologists, and durable medical equipment providers. *See Chapter 3 for more information about CPT codes.*

It has become standard to provide payment based on these codes since the inauguration of medical insurance. Medical coding converts vast amounts of patient, provider, and service information into universally accepted codes. Today, an MIB electronically sends nearly all medical billing claims (each on a CMS 1500 form) to a clearinghouse, which is a company that sends and receives claims electronically for insurance companies. Clearinghouses have contracts with hundreds of insurance carriers and will automatically receive, reformat (if necessary), and redistribute claims to the proper carriers (also known as payers). The clearinghouse provides an important service; without it, each biller would need the proper software for each and every insurance company and would need to enter each claim in the required format, which would be impossible to do. Clearinghouses receive their money from various fees from health care providers and medical billing companies; in other words, those who provide medical billing services. These fees usually consist of a one-time billing center set-up fee (a fair average is $300), a one-time set up fee for the provider (around $50), and a transmission fee for every claim (less than $1 a claim; prices vary depending on what service you choose). Some clearinghouses adjust their fees and bill for a flat amount; for example, $200 a month for 500 claims, plus

50 cents for each claim over 500, while some charge a higher set-up fee in exchange for an unlimited number of transmissions. You as a medical biller will be responsible for paying these fees. *Clearinghouses will be described more in chapters 3 and 4.*

Currently, the insurance industry has grown exponentially and, as you probably know, a large portion of a health care provider's income comes from insurance companies. Insurance companies, Medicare, and Medicaid must guard against fraud and abuse and have stringent guidelines to protect their interests. There are many insurance companies in operation today; the number of rules that medical billers need to know is overwhelming. These factors have created a demand for medical billing services.

Most medical providers are not able to spend the kind of time necessary for medical billing, so they hire a specialist in medical insurance claims billing. This was common practice when claims were submitted on paper, but today it is much more common to file claims electronically, which means the claims process is more efficient, and providers can be paid much faster. The advent of electronic billing has opened a new career trend in virtual, or online, work with medical providers outsourcing their claims to medical billing services.

Medical providers will generally seek a medical billing specialist with extensive experience in medical billing, coding, and accounts receivable management. Although training is not mandatory, formal training in medical billing or certification in medical coding will give credibility to your services and is an advantage in obtaining clients. One of the ways you can gain this certification and credibility is through joining medical billing organizations. This next chapter will explore the different organization and credentials available to you as you begin your new venture into the medical billing industry.

Chapter 2

Organizations, Codes, and the Daily Duties of an MIB

While it is not mandatory you join a medical billing association or go to school to study coding, gaining this experience will help you tremendously when you decide to open a medical billing business. It is fairly common for those involved in the medical billing industry to join medical billing-related organizations. Some medical insurance billing professional organizations and networking organizations are listed below. Nearly all of them have online forums and discussion boards where those new to the business can ask questions or find answers for similar problems shared by many medical billers.

Professional Organizations

American Health Information Management Association™ (AHIMA), www.ahima.org

AHIMA boasts 53,000 members, who all enjoy a variety of newsletters; have a legislative voice; have access to professional development through programs, services, and certifications; and receive discounts on education, certification, publications, and information. Members have access to online job postings and can attend local, state, and national conferences and meetings. Annual dues for active members cost about $165 as of the beginning of 2010.

American Medical Billing Association (AMBA), www.ambanet.net/AMBA.htm

AMBA's focus is networking among peers. Members can access continuing education courses through the Internet, training courses, certification exams, information on clearinghouses and insurance carriers, a new medical billing business start-up program, and are invited to attend the annual conference. The membership dues for this organization are $99.

Electronic Medical Billing Network of America, Inc. (EMBN), www.medicalbillingnetwork.com

EMBN is the oldest and largest trade association and school for independent medical billers in America. Its founder is Merlin Coslick, who consults major corporations and private companies nationwide as a broker, coach, and mentor, and the organization offers different levels of membership, depending on the services you want to receive as a member. Members can take a complete training course for certification as well as buy discounted books on setting up your business, along with software and other items. Members also get savings on printing brochures, postcards, fliers, and business cards, as well as live phone support sessions for business development and creation (length is defined by your membership level; for example, a national membership buys you three 30-minute sessions). Membership dues for medical billers range from $125 a year to $215 a year, depending on the level of membership you are interested in purchasing.

Healthcare Billing and Management Association (HBMA), www.hbma.org

HBMA is the only trade association representing third-party medical billers. Members enjoy networking with other MIBs, product and service discounts, government relations/updates, certification programs, and four major membership meetings/conferences annually. Jobs are also posted online for members to view. The membership dues for this organization vary greatly, depending on the level of membership and how many employees your company has. The dues cost anywhere from $170 to $1,460 for businesses with more than 91 employees.

Medical Association of Billers (MAB), www.physicianswebsites.com

MAB's introductory-, intermediate-, and advance-level training programs are approved and licensed by the Commission for Post Secondary Education. Members receive billing and coding assistance, compliance assistance, job placement assistance, medical billing education and training, and custom training, and they can attend local chapter events and a national annual conference. The annual fee for each individual applying to this organization is $115, but the association offers group discounts when more than one employee from a business joins the organization.

Professional Association of Healthcare Coding Specialists (PAHCS), www.pahcs.org

PAHCS is a member support system and communications network dedicated to enhancing the capabilities of health care coders. Members also enjoy community networking and support, and have access to a nationwide network via the Web site. Membership to join PAHCS is $120.

Training and Certification

An AHIMA survey asked employers if they were more likely to hire a candidate with certification; 68 percent reported they would choose one who was certified over one who was not, and 67 percent of those surveyed reported that they earned more money than their peers who did not have certification.

In addition, acquiring formal training in medical billing can help you become familiar with the language and operations of the health care industry. You will learn how to utilize medical billing software, understand government and insurance regulations, become familiar with medical terminology, and work effectively within the health care community. When you approach potential clients, it is important that you understand the specific medical billing needs of their practice.

Medical terminology is something you will need to become familiar with to ensure your business's success. It is a language that is not easily understood and can be very foreign to you and anyone else who does not work in medicine. If you are fluent in medical terminology, then you will know exactly what the tests are that are indicated on the forms given to you; this knowledge of medical terminology is helpful when you are submitting medical billing claims. If you are looking over the day sheets and do not understand the codes, what they are for, and how they are written, then you will have no idea how to collect payment for your client. You will also not know how to tell when there are mistakes in the billing procedures. If you have taken medical billing courses or have received certification, then you will know your medical terminology. If not, this is where work experience comes in. As you work with medical terminology every day, you will understand it or at least know what the terms you use most commonly mean. If you need help learning it now, you can purchase medical terminology books that will enable you to look up words and phrases, and you can learn them this way. You can also look online for courses that will help you become comfortable with medical terminology.

It may be worth your while to obtain formal training in medical billing before you open your own business. Formal training in medical billing can be found at community and junior colleges, as well as from national medical billing organizations. The length of training varies according to the program, but most are no longer than 24 months. Venturing into the medical billing business with no experience may seem foreign if you have no knowledge of terminology.

Formal training is also an excellent way to demonstrate to potential clients that you know what you are doing, and you have taken special classes and obtained certification to ensure you have knowledge of the medical billing business and the health care industry. Many training programs in medical billing overlap with training in medical coding, medical administration, medical transcription, and insurance specialist training. There are a number of self-paced home-study programs available online, and you can also find courses and programs at vocational or technical colleges and schools in your area.

To achieve certificates issued by various organizations, you must demonstrate knowledge in five subject areas:

1. **Terminology**: Medical terminology and administrative terminology

2. **Anatomy and physiology**: Body planes, body systems, and human physiology

3. **Insurers**: Private insurers, institutional insurers, and insurance claims (especially the CMS 1500 form)

4. **Issuing the medical bill**: Family relationships or responsible party, hospital billing, coding, and fee profiles

5. **Laws, rules, and regulations**: Includes the coverage of HIPAA, fraud and abuse, and compliance

Below is a list of different organizations you can receive certification from and what types of certifications each organization offers.

Committee on Accreditation for Health Informatics & Information Management Education

The Committee on Accreditation for Health Informatics & Information Management Education (CAHIIM) is a national, independent accreditation organization for degree-granting programs in health information management (HIM) and health informatics (HI) nationwide. An HIM professional is someone who manages health care data and health care information resources, while an HI professional would develop information systems that support policies and procedures for handling information to ensure overall security requirements, as well as patient privacy requirements.

HIM and HI programs are found at local universities and community colleges across the country. CAHIIM also accredits online/distance learning HIM programs. The CAHIIM Web site lists associate's (two-year) degree programs, as well as four-year and master's degree programs in HIM at **www.cahiim.org/accredpgms.asp**.

Once you have obtained certification by passing an HIM course, you can list the proper credentials awarded by that organization or school after your name, such as on a business card, résumé, or anything else related to your business or occupation. You would list all credentials you have received throughout your medical billing education. For example, if you complete the basic certification course (Certification Coding Associate-CCA) offered by the American Health Information Management Association (AHIMA), your name and credentials would be properly written as Jane Smith, CCA. If you later completed the Certified Coding Specialist – Physician-based (CCS-P) certification course from AHIMA, your name and credentials would be Jane Smith, CCA, CCS-P.

American Health Information Management Association (AHIMA)

AHIMA, which boasts itself as the premiere association of health information management professionals, offers different courses and certificates. The types of certifications and the prerequisites for taking the different certification exams are listed below:

- **Certified Coding Associate (CCA)** — This is an entry-level credential. Becoming a CCA requires a high school diploma, along with a recommended six months of coding experience in a health care setting (like at a hospital or physician's office) or completion of an AHIMA-approved "Coding Basics Program" (listed on the AHIMA Web site, **www.ahima.org**).

- **Certified Coding Specialist (CCS)** — This certification represents advanced coding and analysis skills. In order to become a CCS, you must have a high school diploma and at least three years of coding experience in a hospital setting.

- **Certified Coding Specialist – Physician-based (CCS-P)** — This certifies you to work in specialty centers, group practices, physician-based offices or clinics, and multi-specialty clinics. A CCS-P certification requires a high school diploma and at least three years of coding experience.

- **Registered Health Information Technician (RHIT)** — An RHIT frequently specializes in coding diagnoses and procedures in patient records for research and reimbursement, and uses computer software and applications to analyze patient data for purposes of improving patient care or controlling costs. RHIT certification requires completion of a CAHIIM-accredited two-year associate's HIM program.

- **Registered Health Information Administrator (RHIA)** — An RHIA is someone who is experienced in managing medical records and patient health information. It requires completion of a CAHIIM-accredited baccalaureate (or bachelor's) HIM program.

- **Certification in Healthcare Privacy and Security (CHPS)** — This is the only combined privacy and security credential available in the health care industry. A CHPS certification requires one of the following:

> » A baccalaureate degree plus four years' minimum experience in health care management

> » A master's degree and at least two years' health care management experience

> » An RHIT or RHIA with a baccalaureate or higher degree and at least two years of experience in health care management

- **Certified Health Data Analyst (CHDA)** — This certification means you are specially trained to analyze health data. It requires a baccalaureate degree plus five years' health data analysis experience, or an RHIA certification plus one year health data analysis experience.

- **Cancer Registry Management (CRM)** — This certification is developed in cooperation with the National Cancer Registrars Association (NCRA). The CRM program is designed for those interested in entering the cancer registry profession where they would analyze and manage clinical cancer information. Cancer registrars have the technical and clinical skills and knowledge to sustain aspects of the disease-related data collection systems consistent with administrative, medical, ethical, accreditation, and legal requirements of the health care delivery system.

None of these courses or certifications is necessary to become an MIB, but they will give you an edge when seeking clients. You must take — and pass — an exam (and sometimes a course) in order to become certified for any of these programs through AHIMA. Approved programs are also available for reference at the AHIMA Web site.

AHIMA offers online self-paced programs to help people learn the skills they need in order to become a coding or HIM professional. The recommended pace, according to AHIMA, is to take four clusters of three classes. Each cluster takes about 15 weeks to complete, adding up to about 60 weeks total if you were to take the clusters without time off in between each one. Courses can be accessed 24 hours a day, and you can attend as many classes as you want, when you want, and study at your own pace.

For example, the Coding Basics full program of all four clusters (for a total of 12 classes) costs $2,000, plus the cost of books, which range from $34.95 to $94.95 each. Cluster One consists of three courses: Health Care Delivery Systems (an introduction to the financing, delivery, and organization of health care services); Medical Terminology (how to break medical terms into suffixes, prefixes, and roots and become familiar with definitions and spelling of common medical terms); and Computer Basics in Health Care (the roles computer and the Internet have played in health care, the basics of software and hardware, and the most commonly used applications, including AHIMA's online tools). Cluster Two consists of harder courses, such as Pathophysiology/Pharmacology; Basic ICD-9-CM Coding; and Health Care Data Content & Structure. Cluster Three classes consists of Basic CPT Coding, Medical Office Procedures, and Basic ICD-9-CM coding, and Cluster Four offers courses in more CPT Coding, Reimbursement Methodology, and Professional Practice Experience.

After completing the Coding Basics Program, you would take the exam to become certified as a Certified Coding Associate. The CCA exam fee for AHIMA members is $205. Exam fees for non-members run $45 more, so it is probably worth the $35 to join as a student member (you must be currently enrolled in an AHIMA-approved coding program or in a CAHIIM accredited HIM program, online or at a college). In order to obtain student membership, go to the AHIMA Web site and click on the coding program or college that you are enrolled in.

The AHIMA exam fees do range according to the certification you are trying to obtain; for example, a CCS-P exam costs $320, while an RHIA certification exam costs $230. The AHIMA Web site also lists exam prep sites for each certification, along with a list of recommended resources for exam preparation, sample test questions, and passing scores for each certification exam.

Healthcare Billing and Management Association (HBMA)

The Healthcare Billing and Management Association (HBMA) offers certification as a Certified Medical Billing Associate (CMBA) and as a Certified Healthcare Billing and Management Executive (CHBME).

According to the HBMA, a CMBA is an ideal certification for managers of medical billing companies. To apply for a CMBA certification, you must first be an employee of an HBMA-member company. (In other words, if you own a medical billing company, it must be a member of HBMA; if you do not own one but work for one, your employer must belong to HBMA). Initial certification is earned by 30 hours of credit, and to maintain certification every year after, you must complete ten credit hours annually. It costs $200 for the initial CMBA application, in addition to paying $100 each year to maintain certification. Up to 60 percent of the required credit hours can be earned by attending HBMA-sponsored programs, including annual meetings, educational conferences, and regular HBMA meetings (local, regional, and national). Each hour of attendance/instruction equals one hour of credit. Credits can also be obtained by serving as an HBMA committee chairperson (three credit hours) or writing articles for HBMA publications (two credit hours for each article). Forty percent of your credits may be earned by attending HBMA-approved educational programs (many are hosted by other billing and coding organizations), and/or 20 percent of credits may be earned through independent study. You can receive up to four credits for writing a positional paper or case study with a focus on the medical billing business. The positional paper or case study must present a problem logically and offer a solution; some examples of topics might be operations workflow, contract negotiation, employee benefit packages and incentives, finances, and new and existing information systems technology. There is no test for certification: Certification is awarded upon completion of classes, attending programs and classes, and independent study. For more information, go to **www.hbma. org/account/files/certification/CMBA2009.pdf**.

A CHBME certification is specially designed for medical billing executives; applicants must be current HBMA members. At least 60 percent of the total credits earned must be obtained through HBMA educational sources. Sixty hours of credit is required for initial CHBME certification (by listing HBMA annual conferences, state and regional HBMA meetings, compliance meetings, Web casts, and so on attended over the past few years, for example). In order to maintain certification, 20 credits must be earned annually, maximum 40 percent from HBMA district learning, and at least 60 percent from HBMA educational sources. Failure to maintain certification means that you would have to re-apply for a new certification. The initial CHBME application fee is $350, and the annual certification maintenance fee is $150. There is no test for the CHBME certification, just HBMA membership and participation in billing industry educational programs, as outlined above.

American Medical Billing Association (ABMA)

A Certified Medical Reimbursement Specialist (CMRS) is certified by the American Medical Billing Association (AMBA) (**www.ambanet.net**) as a person who is skilled in facilitating the claims payment process from the time service is rendered until the balance is paid. AMBA's online Medical Billing Course (**www.medicalbillingcourseonline.com**) is designed to educate the biller on starting and running a medical billing business, and there is an exam at the end of the course. The course costs $325, and a free download demonstration of a class is available. The online exam consists of more than 700 questions and is an open-book exam, so you may use any material needed to research the answers. Most test takers utilize the study guide, a medical dictionary, an ICD-10 code book, a CPT-4 code book, and a health insurance handbook. Students must score 85 percent or more on the test to receive certification as a CMRS.

All of these different certifications will mean more to you as you read and review the material from the different professional organizations. Check each organization's Web site for more information and for guidance as to which certification to pursue, depending on where you want to work and what area of medical insurance billing (if any) you would like to specialize in. One organization may be recommended more highly to you than the others from those already working in the field. If you are comfortable joining that organization based on recommendations from current members, that is the best way to go. While it is not necessary, you will want to obtain certification to show that you are serious about your career and to show your potential clients that you understand the business.

Once you have decided whether to receive extra training or gain additional certifications, you will need to discover what the average MIB does in a day. The next section covers what you as a medical biller will typically experience in your daily work.

A Day in the Life of a Medical Insurance Biller

The following is a typical day in the life of a medical insurance billing professional. Once you have reviewed it, you will have an idea of some of the work that an MIB does. Your day can be much more hectic and could consist of more than the following:

1. Enter all patient information from each physician's day sheet (be sure to include the referring physician and add new insurance carriers) to your database.

2. Enter CPT and ICD-10 codes (International Classification of Diseases, 10th Revision; a system of coding developed by the World

Health Organization) from the day sheets and superbills. *These codes are explained in more detail in Chapter 3.* Your software will automatically fill in the amounts charged for each procedure.

3. Submit claims electronically to insurance carriers (such as Well-Point, UnitedHealthcare, Anthem, BlueCross BlueShield, Medicare, Medicaid, and so on).

4. Review the audit report, which is a list of which claims have cleared and which have errors and have been returned (this is received in your morning e-mail); review and correct any errors listed, and resubmit the rejected and corrected claims.

5. Print and mail paper claims to insurance companies that do not accept electronic claims.

6. Check on past due claims by calling insurance carriers; most of these calls are for paper claims because audit reports contain status of e-mailed claims.

7. Post payments to each patient's account. Your software program will help you determine which charges have not been paid and which ones have been paid.

8. Use your software program to print aging reports; review patient accounts to determine which are behind in payments.

9. Print advertisement newsletters, brochures, or postcards to mail to potential clients, and follow up on the ones previously mailed (you may choose to do this just one day a week, instead of every day).

This is a small example; you can be assured a medical insurance biller's day is much more complicated than it sounds.

A doctor completes a day sheet every day, which is a list of all the patients seen by the doctor that day. This day sheet consists of:

• The date

- File number

- Patient name

- Services that are being billed

- Charges — fees charged for office visits (may be more than one fee if more than one treatment/procedure/service is done)

- Diagnosis

- Balance forward (for each patient)

Procedural coding is a way to describe medical services and procedures performed when a patient visits a doctor's office. The medical and insurance industries have standardized procedural codes that they follow for billing purposes. It is crucial to know the proper billing codes; if you do not, billing will be a nightmare, and many claims will be rejected.

Once a doctor has treated and diagnosed a patient, he or she will sign off on his or her day sheet, marking everything that was done for the patient. After this, the doctor needs to be paid; this is where the MIB comes in.

The doctor must submit the following information to the insurance company (but it will go to you, the MIB, first):

- The date the patient was seen

- The correct codes for completed services/procedures

- The fees charged by the doctor for his or her services

All codes can change at any time for any reason, so you must stay up-to-date with all changes. Codes are the key to a successful claim. The codes will tell you and the insurance company if someone is a new patient; whether someone has already visited the medical practice and been evaluated; what has been done; what needs to be done; what treatment needs to be given; who needs X-rays; and much more information.

Claim Cycle

This is another important aspect of your day as an MIB because it is essentially what gives you the business to keep busy. Below is the cycle a claim will go through when it is submitted for payment:

1. The claim starts when the patient goes to the doctor.

2. The patient shows his or her medical insurance card at the doctor's office. The doctor then checks every service, test, diagnosis, and other similar services that he or she has done to the patient or ordered for him or her on the day sheet/superbill.

3. The doctor's office or the MIB (you) submits the claim electronically to the patient's insurance company. The claim will be rejected if there are any errors.

4. The insurance company verifies that all services completed are covered; if not, the claim is rejected.

5. The insurance company will determine the "allowed charge," meaning the maximum amount the insurance company will pay for the claim.

6. The patient's deductible is brought in to the claim along with the deductible amount and the patient's co-insurance payment (the deductibles must be met before the insurance will pay for any services; insurance co-pays must be made at time of service).

7. The explanation of benefits (EOB) report is completed and printed. Insurance carriers use EOBs to summarize details of a submitted claim and explain reimbursement details. All EOBs contain basically the same information: patient's name/relationship to the insured; services given, dates of service, and total charges; exclusions/remarks about reason for denial; amount of total charges covered; deductible amounts due for each service; percentage of allowed balance paid; and required provider adjustments.

8. Once all forms are read and signed, and the agreement of payment is made, the payment is sent.

Avoiding Rejected Claims

Claims are rejected for many reasons. Once you receive your daily report, you will need to find the mistakes and correct them. You do not want this to happen often because it takes time and effort to correct them. It will be easier to submit claims correctly the first time than to have to revise them and re-submit them. You will need to make sure the doctor's diagnosis is right and submitted correctly in the claim as well. Remember, insurance carriers are great at denying claims, so do your best to not give them a reason to do so.

Here are some reasons why claims get rejected; if you remember to avoid these reasons, you might have a chance of keeping your claims clean:

- Incomplete diagnosis

- Wrong group number

- Confusing diagnosis

- Service and/or treatment that was provided to the patient is not covered by insurance carrier

- Wrong date

- Wrong CPT codes

- Questions left unanswered

- No ICD-10 code given

- Column for fee has been left blank

- Wrong patient information

With insurance companies, you need to be stern, not rude, and let them know you know what you are talking about. It is like a game; if they know they can trick you, they will do it. Insurance carriers can be difficult to deal with, but not always. If you do not receive a reply, then you need to follow up to see what is going on; sometimes claims get lost, and you will not know it for a while.

When submitting claims, here are ways get your claims paid as soon as possible:

- Be accurate

- Send claims from same day, from most expensive to least expensive

- Do not send additional paperwork unless required or requested

Other Service Options

Aside from the information listed above detailing what an MIB does in a standard day, you can choose what services you would like to offer. Some of the services you can offer your clients include doing their accounting as well as submitting reports that include a breakdown of everything you or your clients have billed for in the past month, or however often you and your client agree on sending in reports. Your No. 1 priority will be submitting claims; this is why you are opening your medical billing business, so it is one of the major services you will be offering. Some clients prefer to hire an MIB to do their medical billing and their accounting. As long as your software can support other functions beyond medical insurance billing, you can offer these services to your clients.

Accounting is another task that health care providers commonly outsource, especially if they have trouble hiring someone or training someone to handle this. All this comes into play when you have decided to become a full-practice MIB, which means you have extended your business to cover practice management. You get to choose what range of services you would like to provide because it is your business, your clients, and your time.

Medical billing practice management typically includes any or all of the following:

- Analysis of audit and medical codes

- Annual analysis of billing costs

- Customized reports

- Electronic fund transfer service

- Third-party collection services

- Computer backup services

- Bookkeeping/accounting services

- Appointment scheduling/reminders

- A wide range of monthly reports

These monthly reports could be reports that show the number of patients the client saw for the month, which bills were paid that month and how many have outstanding balances, or the number of the client's patients who were admitted to the hospital that month. There are almost unlimited options for what kind of reports you could provide each month. Sandy Irving, the president of Access Medical Services, explains how she got into the medical billing industry, as well as the type of services she chooses to offer clients.

Now that you are familiar with the services you will be offering clients, as well as what you typical day will entail, it is time for you to become comfortable with the details of the medical billing industry.

CASE STUDY: ACCESS MEDICAL SERVICES

Sandy Irving
President, Access Medical Services

My husband relocated for work in 1993 so we moved from Maryland to South Carolina. I needed to start over in a new career, and I decided I wanted to start my own business. I researched my options, and even though I had no experience in medical billing, I did have business and computer skills. In 1993, I purchased a medical billing "opportunity" package for $6,000 from a company that is no longer in business.

I took coding and medical terminology courses at the local technical college. I had a CPC certification from AAPC but did not re-certify. Because I have so much experience now, and I hire certified billers and coders, I do more management. In the beginning of my MIB career, having had coding and medical terminology courses helped me establish credibility in the market. Coding and billing courses help when learning a new medical specialty or attempting to appeal insurance claim denials.

My company offers full billing services, insurance and patient billing, patient scheduling, limited electronic medical records (EMR), automatic router generation, and full online access to accounts from my secure server. An EMR is a computerized legal medical record of each patient's care, treatment, medication, and services prescribed and received.

Over the past 16 years, the medical billing industry has become more regulated. It is now harder to get insurance companies to pay for claims. The HIPAA regulations, designed supposedly to reduce paperwork, have actually made it harder for us to file claims and obtain payments.

Advice that I have for those just starting their own medical billing business is having medical terminology and medical coding experience. Doing billing in a medical office for about a year is helpful. Getting a practical medical billing certificate from a technical college is also very helpful. You must be detail-oriented, computer-oriented, and have good management skills to succeed in this business. Do not fall for the ads that say, "Work two hours a day in your pajamas from home and get rich." You must be dedicated to working many hours to make a success of any business. Medical billing is highly regulated, hard work.

Chapter 3

Medical Billing Reference Materials/Specifics

N ow that you have a better idea of what a profession in the medical billing industry entails, you must familiarize yourself with the materials you will need to do your job successfully. An important component of the medical billing industry is a form of software called a clearinghouse. This important program will help ensure you submit claims accurately the first time, making sure you clients receive payment as quickly as possible, and send these claims to the appropriate insurance carriers. Another important concept you should familiarize yourself with is the thousands of codes you will use on claims you submit to insurance carriers. It would be impossible to memorize these codes, especially because they are revised on a regular basis, so it is imperative you have the most current research materials available in regard to coding to you so you can process your clients' claims efficiently.

Reference Materials

Working in the medical field means you will be exposed to professional terminology, which may be unfamiliar to you. Rest assured, it can be researched and learned. Programs, classes, and books will help you learn medical terminology. Aside from learning the terminology, the thousands of CPT codes you will be working with are updated yearly so you will need to have guides and reference materials on hand so you can quickly look up any word or code you do not understand; this can help eliminate errors when filing claims. The standard guide for physicians (which you will also need for reference) is the ICD-10, the *International Statistical Classification of Diseases and Related Health Problems, 10th Revision*. This book lists all coding of signs, symptoms, and diseases as categorized by the World Health Organization (WHO). There are more than 155,000 different codes listed.

Other providers have their own manuals, so you will want to purchase them if you choose to bill for a provider in that medical specialty. Some examples are the *Diagnostic & Statistical Manual of Mental Disorders, 4th Edition, Revised (DSM-IV-R)*, for psychologists and psychiatrists, and the dental manual, *Current Dental Terminology, (CDT) 2009-2010*. You should also have the CPT manual, *Current Procedural Terminology*, which is maintained by the AMA. This manual lists all of the diagnostic, medical, and surgical services for which you might be billing.

These guides can be found online at bookstores such as Amazon.com, Inc. **(www.amazon.com),** or specialty medical information supply Web sites such as Ingenix™ **(www.shopingenix.com)**. Ingenix offers printed materials and CD-ROMs, which may be easier to reference as you are billing claims. These guides offer the standard reference materials listed above, as well as coding specific to certain providers (hospitals and durable medical equipment), medical billing information, pricing, and HIPAA compliance. The cost for these materials varies but is usually around $100 per reference guide. If you decide to buy certain reference materials, make sure you are choosing the essentials for your business and the much-needed reference guides as books or CD-ROMs, whichever is more convenient for you. Consider purchasing both books and CD-ROMs for your employees.

Medical Coding

Coding is one of the most important areas to a medical billing professional. While you do not need to memorize all of the codes you will be using on claims you submit to insurance companies, it would be beneficial to familiarize yourself with the most common codes you will be using, depending on the specialty of the doctors you provide services for. This section will cover the types of codes you may be working with as an MIB.

It is important to note that as a medical biller, you are not allowed to change codes that the provider has written without first checking with the medical provider's office. If you think something has been coded incorrectly, first call and discuss the coding with your client or the coder. If you change the code without the provider's permission, you could be opening yourself up to a malpractice suit. Your client, the medical provider, is responsible for making the final coding decision. If he or she agrees to a change that you have recommended, obtain that change in writing and keep it as a record to protect yourself in case of further discussion. The first set of codes this book will cover are Current Procedural Technology, or CPT, codes.

Current Procedural Technology (CPT) codes

CPT codes are five-digit numeric codes that refer to a system of procedures, supplies, and services a doctor performs on a patient during an office visit. These codes were developed by the American Medical Association. The entire group of codes is called the HCFA Common Procedure Coding System (HCPCS), pronounced "hickpicks." The physician or a certified coder is responsible for assigning these codes, usually at the time of the patient visit. You as an MIB need to know enough about codes to be familiar with them so you can show prospective clients that you do understand their business. You should at least study the codes associated with the medical specialties you intend to cover; for example, if your clients will be general practice and family physicians, know the common diagnostic and procedural codes, at least for evaluation and management (codes 99200 to 99499, according to the list below). If you take on a surgeon's medical insurance billing, in order to be familiar with that practice's codes, you should have some knowledge of codes 10000 to 69999. These are surgery codes.

There is a CPT book that lists all 7,000 codes. These codes are revised annually and published by the AMA. There are two levels of codes that are currently used. The first level comprises six sections; each one lists hundreds of different procedures.

The following is an overview of the six sections of the Level I CPT codes. These top-level numeric codes are the most commonly used and describe doctors' services, visits, and procedures:

Evaluation and Management codes	99200 to 99499
Anesthesiology codes	00100 to 01999
Surgery codes	10000 to 69999
Radiology, Nuclear Medicine, and Diagnostic Ultrasound codes	70000 to 79999
Pathology and Laboratory codes	80000 to 89999
Medicine codes	90000 to 99199

Level II consists of five-digit alphanumeric codes related to durable medical equipment, chemotherapy, and medical supplies. Some examples are codes for prosthetic supplies, vision services, hearing services, chiropractic services, orthotic supplies, prosthetic supplies, and for pathology and laboratory supplies. An example of a Level II CPT code is E0105 for a cane, three- or four-pronged, and includes canes of all materials.

Most physicians use no more than a few dozen of these codes because of their specialty in one area of medicine. Using these codes seems pretty straightforward, but MIBs do need to know about procedural coding and the use of modifiers, which can increase your expertise as a professional MIB.

Modifiers are two-digit supplemental codes for certain types of services and procedures that are added to the CPT code, such as for repetitive care (for a chronic medical condition), concurrent care (more than one physician attending a patient), when a procedure or service was reduced or increased, or when only part of a service was performed. The correct modifier can add to a physician's income because insurance companies pay a higher fee for some services. Modifiers follow the decimal point at the end of the CPT code. For example, the diagnosis for a fracture at the base of the skull is 801; if you add to that a diagnosis of a closed fracture with cerebral laceration and contusion, which is .1, the diagnosis for these combined conditions would be 801.1.Many physicians are not familiar with modifiers and will not know to add these modifiers to their codes. Learning about these modifiers will help your clients earn more money by modifying their codes to reflect their services more accurately.

ICD-10 codes

The *International Statistical Classification of Diseases, Tenth Revision (ICD-10), Clinical Modification (CM)* (ICD-10 CM), is a coding system for medical diagnoses and procedures (as compared to CPT, which describe services provided to patients). The ICD-10 CM refers to the modified, or latest codes, but the terms are interchangeable (ICD-10 or ICD-10 CM). ICD-10 codes were developed by the World Health Organization (WHO) and are also updated annually; WHO provides a major update of the ICD codes every ten years.

ICD-10 codes describe signs, symptoms, and characteristics of injuries, accidents, and illnesses on an international level to facilitate medical reporting and medical research. In other words, ICD-10 codes relate to the diagnosis, or what is ailing the patient. A claim can be rejected if the wrong ICD code is entered. It is not necessary to memorize all of the ICD codes, but it is necessary to have the code books and to know how to look up the codes, which are in numeric and alphabetic order.

The ICD-10 Coding Manual consists of two volumes. Volume I is a numerical list of diseases and disorders of the body systems, beginning with 001.0 through 999.9. The codes are three- to five-digits long, and the longer the number, the more specific the code is about the diagnosis. For example, the code for back pain is 724.5. Volume II is an alphabetic listing of diseases.

Other ICD-10 codes are V codes and E codes (included in Volume 1). V codes are assigned by a health care provider when a patient is seen for a reason other than disease or injury; for example, a preventive, or well-baby, checkup is designated with a V code as a diagnosis — the ICD-10 code for a well-baby checkup is V20.2. An E code is assigned to describe an external cause of poisoning, injury, or other adverse reaction affecting a patient's health. An example of an E code is 814.00, which is used to describe a fracture of the carpal bones.

MIBs need to know these codes, or at least have the coding manual, in order to input the codes properly for billing. Diagnosis codes greatly improve the efficiency of automated insurance claims because computers read the codes and match them to common procedures and fee schedules. A health care provider needs to use the most specific level of coding possible, usually a four- or five-digit code instead of a three-digit code.

Once the MIB receives the day sheet with the appropriate codes, he or she will need to submit his or her claims to a clearinghouse.

Clearinghouses

An MIB electronically sends each medical claim to a clearinghouse, a company that checks claims, sorts them, and sends them on to the various insurance companies for processing. After the clearinghouse electronically sends all claims to the proper insurance company, it notifies you of each claim's status via a daily audit report. You will use a clearinghouse to catch errors, get claims paid faster, and make the entire claims filing process easier. Claims get paid faster when filed electronically through a clearinghouse and when reviewed electronically by a clearinghouse.

A clearinghouse works with your medical billing software to create an electronic claim that is transmitted to your clearinghouse account. The clearinghouse then "scrubs" each claim, checking each claim for mistakes based on specific requirements of each carrier/insurance company, and either accepts or rejects the claim. Each accepted claim is then securely transmitted to the payer (the insurance company). Clearinghouses have established security connections with insurance companies that meet strict HIPAA standards so claims are transmitted safely. A message is then sent back to the clearinghouse from the payer, notifying it of the claim's status (accepted or rejected), and the clearinghouse will notify the biller (you) of each claim's status. For each claim accepted, the physician will receive payment, along with an EOB. You can correct and re-submit all rejected claims, and you are not charged for doing so.

There is no cost to the person or company submitting the claims; only the payer is charged for accepting the claim. Clearinghouses charge up to $300 for membership and up to $50 per doctor (the doctors you file for need to be included).

Most insurance companies do not have the capacity or the manpower to receive and process millions of claims daily from millions of health care providers, so an electronic clearinghouse is an efficient, reliable method of sending claims to insurance companies. Clearinghouses provide claims centralization, standardization, and secure transmission to insurance companies (payers).

You will most likely be billing many different insurance companies for claims, so using a clearinghouse will save you lots of work by organizing claims and sorting them according to which insurance companies they should be sent to, and by electronically reviewing each one for errors one last time. A clearinghouse will significantly reduce reimbursement time and will reduce or eliminate time you spend on the phone discussing medical billing claims errors. If an error is found, the claim is sent back to you, the MIB, for correction. You can correct the error quickly and resubmit the claim. Clearinghouses do not correct errors on claims; they just find them.

Electronic data interchange (EDI) is the process whereby the biller (you) sends claims electronically to the clearinghouse, and the clearinghouse reports back with the claim status. Reports from the clearinghouse will notify you of the total amount of claims and dollar amount forwarded to each payer; all the payers included in the batch the clearinghouse received from you; and claims that were forwarded manually (if any) to a specific payer.

Clearinghouses charge for their services; fees may include a start-up fee, a monthly flat fee, or a per-claim transaction fee. Some clearinghouses charge 35 cents for each claim, while others charge a monthly fee of about $50 per account. *Fees for clearinghouses will be discussed in Chapter 4.*

Clearinghouses are able to meet the specific data transmission requirements of every single insurance company that accepts electronic claims. You would need to communicate electronically with hundreds of insurance companies to perform this task on your own; by using a clearinghouse, you only have to communicate with a single entity in order to complete your medical billing duties.

The characteristics of a good clearinghouse are as follows:

- It should include many or all of the national carriers.

- The software will have medical billing software that is compatible with the type of software that your business uses (call and ask the clearinghouse or check its Web site).

- It already has a relationship with each of the insurance companies that you regularly bill (see the list on the clearinghouse's Web site).

- The program has a monthly fee and a contract that is easy to exit.

- It offers advanced features that your business might need as it grows (claim status reports, eligibility verification, sent file status, payment processing, and transaction summaries).

After you have chosen a clearinghouse to perform your medical billing, you will need to obtain the start-up forms you need to submit your claims.

Start-Up Forms Needed

Below is a list of the start-up forms that you will need to complete to start your medical billing business. Most clearinghouses will provide MIB companies with all the forms they need to submit claims. Today, most claims are filed electronically, so beyond the initial start-up forms and contracts required by the clearinghouse, you will not need any more paper forms. The only time you will need paper forms is for those claims that need to be filed by paper, in which case you will print the claim forms instead of sending them electronically.

Start-up forms required by your clearinghouse:

- **Medical claims processing and billing agreement** — Contract between you and the clearinghouse for services

- **Authorization for credit card charge** — Authorization for clearinghouse to charge your credit card for monthly and other fees

- **Provider enrollment form** — Fill out one for each medical practice/client of yours to enroll them for clearinghouse services

- **Payment agreement** — Clearinghouse fees and due dates are listed here, and you sign this form, agreeing to pay them

- **Start-up form** — A list of what needs to be done to ensure your service with the clearinghouse is up and running

- **Provider information form** — You will need to complete one of these for each of your medical practices/clients to enroll them in the clearinghouse

- **Process form** — A contract between you and the clearinghouse detailing the services you will be using

Miscellaneous forms needed

- **Insurance payer list** — This list is from your clients; it is used by the clearinghouse to obtain authorization from insurance companies to send claims to them

- **Electronic data interchange (EDI) enrollment form** — You agree to the stated provisions for submitting Medicare claims electronically to Health Care Financing Administration (HCFA) or to HCFA's contractors

Claims authorization forms

- **Medicaid electronic claims authorization** — When you sign this form, you are assuming responsibility for all Medicaid claims that you submit and will accept liability for them, and will refund overpayments and any other relevant payments

- **Medicare electronic claims authorization** — This form expresses you assume responsibility for all Medicare claims that you submit and will accept liability for them, and will refund overpayments or other necessary amounts

- **BlueCross BlueShield electronic claims authorization** — When you sign this form, you are assuming responsibility for all BlueCross BlueShield claims that you submit and will accept liability for them, and will refund overpayments and other amounts

- **TRICARE (formerly CHAMPUS) electronic claims authorization** — When you sign this form, you are assuming responsibility for all TRICARE claims that you submit and will accept liability for them, and will refund overpayments and other amounts

All of these forms listed above are required to be filled out and submitted before you begin transmitting any claims. Clearinghouses will not let you use their services until these are all completed and returned.

Before you start processing and submitting claims, you will need to know how to do the following:

- Process claims

- Regulate billing

- Code bills

- Re-submit rejected claims for each health care provider (rules/regulations may be different for each provider)

You will have learned these through taking classes or by working in a medical insurance billing position.

After you become familiar with the coding system(s) you will have to use on a daily basis, it is time to choose which kind of software you will use in your office. There is a multitude of options available for you to choose, so do not feel limited by the ones presented in the next chapter. It is a good idea for you to ask colleagues in the field what software they use and whether they would recommend it to you. Try not to become overwhelmed by all the choices available on the market; it is best to choose software that others in the MIB industry use and trust.

Chapter 4

Software Choices

There are numerous software programs you will need to purchase to run a successful medical billing business. Your list should include a medical claims billing software program (an example is CollaborateMD with a set-up fee of $899; many other programs are listed below); a word processing program, like Microsoft Word (approximately $200); and a financial program, like Quicken (about $100). Make sure the software you buy is user-friendly — it should be easy to learn, use, and operate, with tech support readily available if you need it.

The following section will help you select from an abundance of software programs. You should also be aware that if you are not computer- or software-savvy, you will have a difficult time understanding the software. It is challenging, but it can be explained and understood as long as you are patient enough to learn and gain knowledge. There is usually a phone number on the back of the directions booklet for support in case you need help installing the program or have any questions. The medical billing software is sometimes confusing and hard to understand if you are unfamiliar with it; hopefully you have used medical billing software before if you worked in medical billing. Before obtaining your first client, you should have all of your business equipment (including software) in your office, ready to start work on the first client's bills. Of course, it helps if you know how to run the software and are completely trained and ready to work in the medical billing field. Then you can begin marketing and advertising your services to physicians in your area (while continuing to practice using your new medical billing software).

Make sure the medical billing software you purchase:

- Will allow you to enter patient and insurance information

- Will print monthly reports

- Will keep track of patient balances

- Will back up your files (Backing up your files is crucial; if you do not have your files backed up and something happens to your computer, you can consider all your information gone)

If you are in a network with a medical billing business or association, or belong to a national organization, you can ask what software your colleagues or peers use and if they would be willing to show you how to use it.

Medical Claims Billing Software

The medical billing software is configured to catch any errors, so electronic claims submission is more accurate and is reimbursed quickly. Most software packages give you as many capabilities as you need so that if you expand your services, you will not need to upgrade. These capabilities go beyond just medical claims filing and tracking and may include the following features:

- Automated claims submission

- Real-time adjudication (instant submission to insurance companies with notice of payment or denial in seconds)

- Electronic payment statements

- Comprehensive reporting

- Claims tracking

- Claims control

Many people buy a medical billing software program without knowing much about it and without researching the company thoroughly. This is an unwise move because many medical billing software companies have failed recently. Some of them were fraudulent and did not deliver the training or technical support promised to customers.

Before deciding which software to purchase, look for a medical billing software company that has been in business for a while (more than just a few years), and ask if you can contact some of their customers. Follow through by calling a few customers and asking if the company has provided training on using the software and if it provides efficient technical support and product updates. Some companies also extend themselves to teach medical billing entrepreneurs how to market their services to health care providers, how to win a contract, and how to use their software properly. Some also provide marketing materials for you to mail to prospective clients. These companies are providing a good software program and services for their customers, and you should be aware of the leading software providers and research them first before looking into companies you have never heard of before.

You can usually purchase the software program for a set fee, but some vendors offer what they call a "business opportunity" package for a higher fee. This package might include items like the software, coding books, health care manuals, marketing materials, audio and/or videotapes, and training. A "business opportunity" package is not always a good deal because it may contain services you might never use, such as help with marketing your medical billing business, several hours of extensive technical support, or a very long warranty (which is not good if it is for more than a few years because most computer experts recommend replacing computers every three to five years). Be sure to explore the details of each program. It is up to you to determine whether you want to buy the software only, with or without any extras that the company provides, such as extensive technical support.

Most software programs have a number of features that are useful to medical billing specialists, whether they are working at a provider's office or working remotely as a billing service. These programs handle medical records for the patient's history, procedures, diagnosis, services rendered, and insurance company information. You can purchase medical billing software to install on your computer that will store all your data on your computer, or you can download Web-based software that will encrypt and store all your data online.

Web-based software

The latest in medical billing technology is Web-based medical billing software, which means the application is hosted on a centralized server and there is no software that needs to be installed on your computer. This process involves the biller (you) logging into the Web site of a company that offers this service. Once logged in, you can perform the medical billing function on the site. The page you will see is similar to that of software you have probably already used or currently use. A start-up fee and a monthly subscription fee are usually the only things required to use and access Web-based medical billing software.

One advantage to choosing this kind of software is no matter where your business moves, you will always have access to your Web-based medical billing software because an Internet connection is all you need. The data will not take up any of your hard drive space, and medical billing software maintenance, along with updating and upgrading it, is not required because the Web-based medical billing software company takes care of it. Because purchasing software is not necessary, up-front costs for Web-based medical billing software are generally lower than purchasing software to install on your computer. Web-based medical billing software keeps data secure and reliable.

For example, if you live in a hurricane-prone area of the country, utilizing Web-based medical billing software would be an excellent choice because if your office is damaged and you have to relocate, you can still provide medical billing services to your clients because everything you need is on-line. Your client information and data, links to clearinghouses, and all your reference materials (such as ICD-10 codes) are all readily accessible as long as you know your password.

Some medical billing software programs focus just on medical insurance billing, while others offer a wider range of services, known as medical practice management software programs. This software includes the following functions:

- Appointment scheduling
- Insurance verification (determining patient eligibility)
- Line item and account posting
- Electronic patient statements
- Comprehensive reporting
- Document imaging and storage
- Electronic medical records (EMRs)
- User management
- Claim tracking
- Claim control
- Automatic claims submission

The best billing software for your business is one that is easy to use. The only way to determine that is to try it out yourself. Vendors understand this and will likely be happy to meet your request to try out a product with a free trial period or a free software download.

A traditional software system is one that you run on your own computer, while application service provider (ASP) software has most data processing and storage done at the software company's data center, which is accessed online. This makes it easy for you because you have no software on your computer to worry about. However, if you decide to purchase software to run on your computer, there are countless options available to you.

Traditional software options

Software that you purchase and run on your computer (the traditional software system) will involve a larger purchase cost. Web-based software is usually priced monthly per user (like a lease arrangement).

There is no standard ranking method for medical billing software. Various industry-related Web sites offer software ranking according to users' comments, but just because a few users give their experience a high ranking does not necessarily mean the software program is the right one for you. One site, **www.medicalbillingsoftwarepro.com,** asks users to rank medical billing software. This may be one of the places you look when researching what type of software you wish to buy.

CollaborateMD

This medical billing software touts itself as one of the easiest Web-based medical billing software programs available and states the user can be up and running within a few hours, as opposed to days later with other software packages. The software, database, and clearinghouse connections are maintained through the CollaborateMD (**www.collaboratemd.com**) server, meaning the user requires less time and back-up file space. All data is encrypted, and only authorized users can access it.

This package offers tracking for claims you have already submitted, which helps highlight any rejected claims and decipher why they were rejected. You can edit the rejected claims for resubmission. This package also includes an editing system, which will review your claims for errors before they are sent to the clearinghouse, reducing the number of errors or omissions leading to rejections. The reporting capabilities for CollaborateMD are extensive, including the Electronic Remittance Advice (ERA), a payment explanation from providers that explains their claims payments.

CollaborateMD also offers telephone, e-mail, and internal messaging support services if you have questions. CollaborateMD offers a 30-day moneyback guarantee and is a member of the Better Business Bureau online. It also offers user-led forums, video training, and secure messaging.

AllegianceMD

This company bills itself as having the only medical billing software that has been formulated using artificial intelligence (AI). AllegianceMD (**www. allegiancemd.com**) defines AI as a computer application that studies human actions and translates them so a computer understands them. The translated actions are then used later to make decisions based on your past decisions; target potential glitches; and self-correct. The company states AI streamlines operations by making decisions instantly based on the user's past actions and choices. The AI is purported to scour claims, catch errors, and update frequently to reflect the most current regulations. As with most medical billing software packages, once the claims have been entered, they are ready to file.

This software package is also Web-based, so you can go online and begin using it right away. The program is 256-bit encrypted for security and is also HIPAA-compliant, meaning patients' confidential data is secure. The software is also backed up every 30 minutes, ensuring as little work as possible will be lost.

AllegianceMD's software package includes templates, forms, error alerts, and "ticklers" (reminders of tasks that need to be done). Support features include Quick Help and Hints, live online chats or phone consultations with customer service representatives, and online training. AllegianceMD says its clients choose this software because it is efficient, transparent (clients have the ability to access real-time data all the time), effortless, maintenance-free, and HIPAA-secure.

ClaimTek

This software prepares you to handle not just the medical billing for a physician, but many other aspects in case you decide to expand your services to include practice management. The name of its software is MedOffice, and it offers hundreds of reports you can generate for your clients on a monthly basis. It can be installed on your office computer or accessed online. Because you will not know what kind of medical practice your potential clients will own, it is best to be prepared for them by having software with full medical practice management capabilities. ClaimTek (**www.claimtek.com**) also includes medical billing software and ancillary software programs, including coding software and billing cost analysis software.

ClaimTek has been recognized in national business magazines. The services that you can provide to your physician clients with ClaimTek software include:

- Third-party collections
- Electronic fund transfers
- Billing practice management
- Remote backup services
- Patient well-care services
- Digital scanning and archiving for medical records (for example, electronic document management)
- Software sales, training, and support

Four different programs are available for purchase from ClaimTek, in addition to buying software and support programs separately: the Essential Program, Principal Program, Preferred Program, and the Preferred Plus. Program prices range from about $6,000 and up; all include software, service, marketing, training, and support. More about each of these programs can be found on ClaimTek's Web site.

Some other medical billing software packages to consider (and remember, there are thousands of them on the market, so consider them carefully) are MPMSoft (**www.mpmsoft.com**), Medisoft (**www.medisoft.com**), AdvancedMD (**www.advancedmd.com**), Avisena (**www.avisena.com**), EZ Claim (**www.ezclaim.com**), and NueMD (**www.nuemd.com/medical_ software/medical_billing_software.html**). Some of these are Web-based, while others require software purchases.

Ask for a demonstration when comparing two or three different software packages. Remember to buy software that is capable of growing along with your business.

Affinity Billing evolved from what was originally a software company. Affinity Billing's owner took advantage of technology and his knowledge of the business to develop software a medical billing company could use. Improving the service quality of your medical billing company will always be something you strive for, along with explaining to doctors why your company is the best one to meet their medical billing needs and challenges.

CASE STUDY: AFFINITY BILLING

Yuval Lirov, CEO
Marlboro, NJ
www.affinitybilling.com

A physician friend asked me in 2001 to build him a Web-based system to submit claims. He complained about underpayments and payment delays; he thought that if he had a better mechanism to submit clean claims, his problems would go away. So we built for him Vericle® — a Web-based claims management software that integrated with WebMD℠ (today Emdeon) and scrubbed claims.

As we started to sell our software to other billing companies, and the volume of claims submitted for payment through Vericle increased, we discovered many physicians were unable to get paid in full and on time, even when they submitted clean claims. As we shifted our focus from charge processing to payment processing, we discovered that insurance payers systematically underpay and delay payments using state-of-the-art technology and well-trained personnel to implement sophisticated strategies to underpay providers.

Over the past five years, some specialties lost as much as 20 percent in the allowed payments. Every year, the payers reduce allowed amounts and become more sophisticated in underpaying providers and in conducting post-payment audits, trying to take back money already paid to providers.

As a result, it takes more data and better algorithms to discover underpayment patterns. It also takes many more follow-up calls to the payers to correct the underpayments, which necessitates continuously improved process control to manage follow up teams. The technology supporting such activities evolved from claim scrubbing and submission to payment processing and auditing, to follow-up process management, to complete integration with patient life cycle, including visit scheduling and electronic medical records (EMR or EHR).

Using our system, the biller does not have to waste time analyzing accounts receivable reports. Vericle's "billing network" aggregates claim data and automatically discovers not only incidents of delay and underpayment, but also their patterns. All the biller has to do is follow up on every problem the same day. This way, the billing company using Vericle leaves no claim behind and gets the provider paid in full and on time.

When you get started with your medical billing business, client attraction is going to be your first biggest problem. System switching is painful and expensive; you need to have your answers to the following questions ready: Why should billing be outsourced to you instead of another biller? Will your billing service meet doctors' expectations? How will those expectations be met?

Consistently improving service quality is going to be your next biggest problem. How are you going to measure service quality? How will you solicit client feedback? How will you process it and how will you improve your service?

Always work on perfecting your processes. You need separate processes for marketing, sales, and client enrollments, as well as training, billing, and quality control. You need to have ways to track them, measure their performance, and figure out ways to improve.

You need to think about marketing and sales; set up reliable and scalable processes; hire reliable staff; and make a profit. Do not start your company and do not sign up a single client until you see precisely how much profit you will make and how will you manage your service quality.

Finally, as an MIB, you need to be comfortable with change. Adjusting to change is your third biggest challenge as clients change their priorities, the industry evolves, and the technology doubles its power every 18 months.

Coding and Reference Software

Coding and reference software is useful for researching coding and reference needs. Medical insurance billers have to deal with complex documentation and continual regulatory changes so they may use several reference books every day. If the process of using a reference book is difficult, the quality of medical record coding and/or billing may decrease because billers may not have the time to use references as often as they should. If MIBs have to share reference books, that affects their job productivity. Having references available to them on CD-ROM is one way to make it easy for

MIBs to ensure the accuracy of their work with appropriate, convenient, and up-to-date references. The following are examples of software you may find valuable to your medical billing business:

3M™ Coding Reference Plus Software

This may be the most extensive online reference material available to coders. The 3M Coding Reference Software includes these reference works: *American Hospital Association's Coding Clinic*; *AMA's CPT Assistant*; *Clinical Pharmacology Drug Reference*; *Dorland's Medical Dictionary*; and *Elsevier's Anatomy Plates*. The Coding Reference Plus Software can be added to systems that already have the 3M Coding Reference Software. The Coding Reference Plus Software includes *Coders' Desk Reference* from Ingenix, AHA's *Coding Clinic for HCPS*, *The Merck Manual of Diagnosis and Therapy*; *Faye Brown's ICD-9-CM Coding Handbook; the Dictionary of Medical Acronyms and Abbreviations; Mosby's Diagnostic and Laboratory Test Reference;* and *Dr. Z's Interventional Radiology Coding Reference*. This software can be found at **http://solutions.3m.com/wps/portal/3M/en_US/3M_Health_Information_Systems/HIS/Products/Coding_Reference.**

Medical Coding.Net

This is easily accessible online (**www.medical-coding.net**) and is an expert source for medical coding books, medical coding data files, and medical coding and medical billing software. The products Medical Coding.net offers boast combinations of the best coding information and the best reference functions available. Most products include 12 months of ongoing updates.

RAmEx Ars Medica, Inc.

This company is an international distributor of medical multimedia titles that are useful for billing and coding, medical education, medical training, medical reference, medical diagnosis, and medical library reference. Some

CD-ROM titles include *Data Collection and Analysis for Generating Proce-dure-Specific Practice Expense Estimates* ($1,243) and the *National Correct Coding Initiative (CCI) Reference Tools Including the National Correct Cod-ing Policy Manual for Part B Medicare Carriers* ($600). You can find out more about this company at **www.ramex.com**.

MedeTrac.com

This company specializes in quality discount medical billing and medical coding resources for your professional practice. The Web site (**www.medetrac.com**) offers 2010 coding books for coding for many dif-ferent medical specialties, software, medical dictionaries, medical refer-ences, health service directories, medical terminology resources, medical insurance forms, along with continuing education courses in medical bill-ing and coding.

Labeling Software

Labeling software will help make business mailings much easier. When you start advertising your medical billing business through bulk mailings and surveys, you will probably be mailing them several times each week. *More about this will be described in Chapter 10.* A labeling software program will help you manage all your contacts and their addresses. It will also help you keep track of what you sent to whom, and you will be able to add, delete, or change addresses.

Below are a few options to consider when researching labeling equipment. Remember, this is not an exhaustive list of programs available to you; check with other MIBs in the industry to see what software they use, or perform an Internet search to research more options.

Worldlabel.com, Inc.

Worldlabel.com, Inc. (**www.worldlabel.com/Pages/software.htm**) is a manufacturer of labels that can be used on letter-sized sheets, laser label sheets, and inkjet printer labels. You can find more than 50 standard size label formats here. You can buy label sheets at a huge discount (for example, 30 labels per sheet on standard white matte costs about $89 for 1,000 sheets; about $174 for 2,000 sheets; and about $397 for 5,000 sheets). Labels are similar to the brands available at office supply stores. Worldlabel. com, Inc. Designer Version 5 label software program offers 15 free uses, and you are able to download a free trial. Wordlabel.com, Inc. bills itself as a complete office solution software for your labeling and printing needs. Print and design your own envelopes, mailing labels, address labels, CD labels, and DVD labels. The software has its own database to store personal information and/or address labeling for mail merge (making multiple documents from a single template or merging multiple sources of information — addresses and names, for example — into one template). Software also includes clip art graphics, backgrounds, and textures. You can also import your own graphics and the software supports popular graphic formats.

CAM Development

CAM Development (**www.camdevelopment.com**) offers business card- and label-making software. Its Label Designer Plus software ($40) helps you create professional address, shipping, CD, and DVD labels; labels for your audio tapes, disks, ZIP disks, file folders; and more.

Easy Mail Plus

This company's label software ($50) offers two formats: the Easy Mail Plus database and a free-form address book. You can design your own graphic layout of your business mailing labels. Standard envelope sizes are already defined, so you can select one of these templates or define your own label size to use. This software will back up and save your labels and create custom mailing reports. Visit their Web site (**www.easymailplus.com/features.html**) for more information.

Accounting Software

Another type of software you may wish to purchase is accounting software. You may choose to outsource your medical billing business's accounting and bookkeeping to an accountant, or in the interest of saving money, you may rely on an accounting software program to do this yourself. With the help of software to keep track of income and expenses, you may find this job a little bit easier than you had first imagined.

There are many accounting software programs to choose from and a few of them are listed below.

Peachtree Pro Accounting

Peachtree Pro ($200) is ideal for a small medical billing business with a single user. It has standard accounting tools like accounts payable, accounts receivable, and internal accounting review. It also features business management tools, such as payroll solutions, integration with Microsoft programs, and more than 100 reports and financial statements. First-time Peachtree users get 30 days' free technical support. More about this software can be found at **www.peachtree.com**.

Intuit™ QuickBooks

Intuit QuickBooks Pro 2010 software for a single user costs $180. It is good for your medical billing business because it offers users the ability to print checks, pay bills, track expenses, track customer payments, manage payroll and payroll taxes, track invoices, create purchase orders, and create business reports with a single click. Visit the QuickBooks Web site (**http://quickbooks.intuit.com**) for further information.

Simply Accounting® by Sage/First Step 2010

Simply Accounting's First Step® software is ideal for a single user in a small business like yours. It can prepare invoices, receive payments, write checks, create and customize reports, and store up to two years' financial business history for about $50. Simply Accounting's Sage Pro does all the above, but also handles payroll, tracks projects and budgeting, and integrates with Microsoft programs for about $170 (single user). The Simply Accounting Web site (**www.simplyaccounting.com**) can provide you with more information. Some of these programs also offer other capabilities in addition to accounting:

- Payroll

- Direct deposit

- 401(k) deduction

- Tax table

- W2 forms

- W3 forms

- 940 forms

Clearinghouse Options

This section lists some options for clearinghouses you can use in your medical billing business. *For a refresher of what a clearinghouse does, read Chapter 3.*

MPM-edi Clearinghouse

MPMsoft and MPM-edi Clearinghouse work together, so if you are considering buying MPM software, this might be another reason to do so. It automatically updates your accounting and claim status reports, and error codes are displayed prominently so you will know what is wrong. This software allows you to edit and correct claims online at any time. Support staff is available, and it is affordable at $125/month (for one-on-one claims support) per rendering provider for unlimited claims. MPM-edi Clearinghouse has one of the largest payer lists in the industry and currently transmits electronic claims to more than 1,400 payers nationwide. MPM will add any health-benefit payer with an insurance ID within 72 hours of request. More about this clearinghouse can be found by visiting **www.mpmsoft.com/EDI/clearinghouse_all.htm**.

i-Plexus Solutions

With i-Plexus Solutions (**www.iplexus.net**), payers can be matched using payer names or by payer IDs, and specific claims can be found online by searching by patient name. Claim status can be found for any stage in the EDI cycle; validations can be tailored by customer, payer, specialty, or almost any field on the HCFA form; and changes can be made to errored claims on the Web in real time and immediately cleared to go to the payer clean the first time. This program provides acceptance rates to see how you measure up within your peer group, and the i-Plexus validation engine stops faulty claims sooner, which increases your cash flow.

There are three pricing options available: any payer on their site is free as long as you do not send Medicare, BlueCross BlueShield, or Medicaid claims; a fixed monthly fee of $70 per provider per month (the more providers you send the less the per provider fee); or the per-transaction fee, which starts at 35 cents a claim and goes as low as 15 cents a claim, depending on the volume, but there is a minimum monthly fee of $60 a month if you plan on sending fewer than 172 claims a month.

ZirMed

The ZirMed Web site (**www.zirmed.com**) says they let your claims pass through an extensive system of edits to ensure clean claims are delivered to payers the first time. Their powerful claims tracking feature eliminates lost claims by reporting when payers receive, deliver, and accept your claims. ZirMed's online tools allow you to research, edit, and resubmit your claims quickly if rejections do happen.

Gateway EDI[SM]

GEDI Connect includes unlimited electronic claims and paper claims, individual status claims query, and unlimited eligibility inquiry. This software offers Data Tools, which have the ability to send and receive encrypted files and offer rejection analysis, sent files status, transaction summary, safety net report (which updates the status of re-submitted claims), and claim file reconciliation. GEDI Swift includes all the above, plus unlimited electronic remittance advice (help with submissions), and unlimited secondary claims processing environment (if a patient has a supplementary health insurance policy, it will manage that claim and recoup money for the medical provider that would otherwise be lost). You can read more about this clearinghouse by visiting its Web site (**www.gatewayedi.com**).

After you have purchased the necessary software specific to the medical billing industry, it is time to get your business off the ground and running. The next chapter of this book will describe some of the first steps you should take before starting your medical billing business.

Chapter 5

Starting Your Medical Billing Business

S tarting a medical billing business is going to be one of the biggest accomplishments in your life, and you should start with high expectations to make this business a successful one. Mistakes can and do happen, especially when launching your own business. Just about every one of the medical billing business owners profiled in the case studies included in this book said they have something they wished they would have done differently. Start this business with all your best efforts with the goal of someday sitting back and saying, "I have given this business everything I have, and I have no regrets." Take your time establishing your business, and do not overwhelm yourself.

Diving into the Medical Billing Biz

Medical billing is a year-round business; claims must be filed no matter what happens with the economy or the weather, and patients receive medical care 365 days a year. Someone has to bill the insurance companies for their care.

If you provide physicians with commitment, expertise, knowledge, and consistency, you will find yourself busy and have no shortage of doctors who want your services. Physicians (like everyone else) want to have a choice of whom they should hire to provide their medical billing services. If they are not satisfied with their current medical biller's services, they will look around for another biller. As the U.S. population increases, the number of people seeing physicians will also increase, as well as the number of medical claims that need to be filed with insurance companies. You will have relative job security, as long as you provide quality service at a reasonable price.

Today's physicians utilize a payment method called a superbill (also called a charge slip), and these are filled out by hand or electronically before a patient leaves the doctor's office. Each item listed in the superbill has a corresponding code number, which is what you as the medical biller will be most interested in for billing purposes. The physician checks the box next to each procedure or service he or she has performed on the patient at that visit. Your job is to enter the procedure and diagnosis codes into a CMS 1500 claim form on your computer and send it electronically to the insurance company. Hopefully, you will have lots of procedure and diagnosis codes to enter during your medical billing career.

A large learning curve is involved in the medical billing business. Even if you are familiar with insurance or with the medical/health care field, there is still a lot to learn as a medical billing business owner. This is a problem-solving business — one that requires people skills; marketing skills; some knowledge of technology to know how electronic billing works; and what needs to be done in the case of rejected claims. A medical biller must understand the entire billing process in order to be successful and also ensure he or she does not do anything illegal; mistakes may be considered insurance fraud.

Despite the current debate over health care in the United States and the potential for changes in the manner in which health care is administered, physicians will still need to be paid, and insurance companies will still need to be billed. Medical insurance billers will always be needed, so your future in this field looks great.

Researching Your Business Options

When you start out in this industry, you can begin by focusing on medical insurance billing for a few health care providers, and you can eventually cover all patient billing, delinquent claims, and practice management if you decide to expand your business this way. You may choose to specialize in a single area of billing, such as for cardiology or urology, and expand your services in this way. If you choose to specialize your practice and have obtained the corresponding certification from the Professional Association of Healthcare Coding Specialists (PAHCS), you will only provide medical billing services for practices within your chosen specialty. Some MIBs prefer to focus on medical insurance billing, while some choose to expand into medical practice management.

Medical practice management

Medical billing is part of a larger business known as medical practice management, which is when a medical biller expands his or her practice to help physicians manage their entire medical practice. However, this is not something you have to do; you can start out in medical billing and see where your new career takes you. If you enjoy the work and get the opportunity to help a physician manage other aspects of his or her practice, you may want to take advantage of this opportunity. Then again, you may decide you want to stay focused on medical billing, and there is nothing wrong with that.

Medical practice management comprises services beyond medical billing. If you decide to expand your MIB business into medical practice management, then you will most likely offer your clients services such as:

- Annual analysis of billing costs

- Customized reports

- Monthly reports on receivables and aging

- Insurance charge analysis

- Practice analysis

- Managed care analysis

- Insurance reimbursement analysis

- Third-party collection services

- Electronic fund transfer services

- Back-up services (storing client data at a remote, secure location)

Medical practice management is simply offering more extensive services beyond medical insurance billing in order to increase your income and to help clients with their needs. You may not even think of offering more than medical insurance billing services until you are made aware of a client's particular needs beyond those you provide, and then you may be in a position to act upon them and help.

Starting Your New Business Venture

Like anything else in life, starting a medical billing business is risky. There is always the "what if." What if I do not get enough clients to pay my business expenses and have a little profit as well? What if I cannot find any well-trained employees? What if I cannot market my medical billing business to physicians as well as I need to in order to get new business? What if I cannot pay my employees? What if I make mistakes? What if I make a big mistake and a physician terminates our contract? What if I am just not ready to own my own medical billing business?

Starting a business is not a decision to be made lightly; you must carefully plan for this new endeavor, down to the smallest detail. Planning will help eliminate some of those business risks and let you see what is to be expected. First of all, research the medical billing business to determine if another medical billing company is needed or will be useful — not only in your geographic location, but nationwide. Thanks to the Internet, you will be able to advertise your business online and solicit business across the country.

Consider the people you will have to deal with in this business, all the pressures you will be under, the rejections from insurance companies, and the clients you will have to deal with. Starting a new business is risky because you will not know if you can handle it until you are in the middle of it. One of the most important issues you will need to deal with immediately will be the bills you will be forced to pay until your business starts bringing in money to support itself.

Starting a medical billing business has many rewards as well as risks. Many roadblocks will get in the way of your business and if you are able to work through them, you may have the strength, knowledge, and perseverance needed to operate a successful medical billing business. The first of many steps you need to take when establishing your new medical billing business is deciding what you will call your business.

Choosing a business name

There are many ways to choose a name for your medical billing business. One of the more popular methods is to use some sort of medical-related term or support term, such as Access Medical Services, one of the case studies that is listed in this book. *See the end of Chapter 2 for this Case Study.* You could also use a regional term including your city or county, or if you hope to gain clients throughout the country, "National" or "Nationwide" is a possibility. You could try a superlative term, such as "Best."

When you name your business, make sure you have thought about it because you do not want to wake up one day and say, "I really don't want it to be called My Medical Billing Business anymore." Most businesses do not make a habit of changing their name because it is not good business sense.

If you are not consistent when it comes to your business's name, your clients may then wonder if you can be consistent with their account. Naming your business is a significant decision and should not be taken lightly; this name will stick with you for as long as you are in business.

When naming your medical billing business, think of what your business stands for. Some of the attributes that might or should be included are:

- Accurate billing
- Dependable/responsible/reliable
- Knowledgeable
- Helpful

If you plan to target a specialized area of health care, that could be included in the business name, such as "Dental Billing Associates" or "Neurology Claims Filing." Many people choose to insert their surname into the business name so providers might more easily remember them and their services. Think about your surroundings. What is your city or town known for — a mountain, a large river, or an annual national sporting event? Your goal is to choose a name that stands out from the competition, conveys the quality of your service, includes descriptive words, and is memorable.

Remember: You will build a medical billing business Web site with your new name, and if it is a long name, think twice, because it could be hard to remember. You can imagine answering the phone "Thank you for calling Columbus's No. 1 Mighty Medical Billing Company — You Cannot Go Wrong With Us Doing Your Billing." That will help you consider a shorter business name — something easy to understand, like "Mountainside Billing." Make sure it is not too hard for your potential clients to understand your business name over the phone.

Once you have chosen a name, you will need to determine whether it is in use by another company or entity. Perform a business entity search online to accomplish this task. Most states have a Web page devoted entirely to this process. The Web page also includes information on how to register your new business name.

After you have chosen a name for your business, contact the secretary of state's office in your state to register a new business name, or they will direct you to the correct office in order to do so. Your legal name is the one under which your company is legally organized, so it is also the name under which you will pay your business's federal income tax. The business will need to have an established address, and there will be a fee for registering your business.

In some states, each business must continuously maintain a "registered agent" and a registered office. The registered agent is the person whom the state will contact for service of process, notice, or demand required or permitted by law to be served on the business entity. In other words, your name and business address must be kept on file and updated in case the state needs to contact you for any legal matters concerning your medical billing business, which the state has the right to do.

"Doing business as" (DBA)

DBA is a business name, also called a trade, assumed, or fictitious name. For example, if your medical billing business is a sole proprietorship (which will be explained in the next section), then its legal name is the same as your name. To conduct business or open a bank account under a business name (one that is different than your name), you will need to register it as a DBA.

If you are a sole proprietor and desire to create and establish a business name that is different from your name, then either register an assumed name (DBA) or incorporate your business. *See how to incorporate later in this chapter.* If your business remains a sole proprietorship and you file a DBA, you are only assigning yourself a business name; for example, Jane Doe DBA Star Medical Billing.

It is important for you to remember and realize that having a DBA does not protect you from any business obligations or business debt. When you incorporate a business, you are setting up an entity that is separate from you, so a having a different business name in that case is more feasible.

Also be aware that many businesses online offer to handle the paperwork required for filing and registering a business DBA. You can complete the process yourself on your state's Web site, most likely the secretary of state's Web site, but this may vary from state to state. If you feel that you are swamped in paperwork and cannot handle the additional paperwork required, then this is an option for you if you do not mind the costs (which, again, vary according to the company that you choose).

Trademark Registration

Once you have established a business and are happy with the name you have chosen, then you can take the business name to the next level by protecting it with a registered trademark.

A trademark is indicated by a raised abbreviation ™ after a company or product name, and it shows ownership. It is mainly a way to distinguish and/or identify one company or product name from another. The U.S. Patent and Trademark Office (**www.uspto.gov/main/trademarks.htm**) provides more information about trademarks as well as electronic filing of trademark applications. You can search the trademark database to be sure your company's name is not already taken (**http://tess2.uspto.gov/bin/gate.exe?f=login&p_lang=english&p_d=trmk**).

If you do not register your medical billing company's name, then anyone can use it.

After you have chosen your business's name, you will need to decide what structure your business will have. Some of the options for business structures include sole proprietorships, partnerships, and corporations, just to name a few. This next section will cover all the business structures available to you.

Selecting a Business Structure

There are many factors to consider when deciding the structure of your new medical billing business because the structure will affect your income, liability and tax requirements. More formal structures such as corporations seem to offer less risk to your personal assets; however, there are more requirements, fees, and expenditures of time and effort to maintain a corporation. If you are starting up your business and starting out small, the simplest and least expensive business structure is the sole proprietorship. You can change your business's structure as the business grows if you decide to add a partner or incorporate your business. When you decide to expand your business, your attorney and financial advisors can advise you as to the best way to structure your business.

When starting your business, you will need to obtain an employer identification number (EIN). You will need this number for tax purposes, business licenses, or for obtaining a bank loan or business bank account. You can apply online for one through the IRS at **www.irs.gov/businesses/ small** if your business is located in the United States or U.S. territories. You will need a valid social security number for the application. After you complete the online application and your information has been verified, you will receive your EIN immediately. After you receive your EIN, you will need to:

- File a fictitious owner affidavit if your company name is different from your own name (this informs the government and the public that your business will operate under a name other than your own; file the form at your county recorder of deeds' office, or government equivalent).

- Decide on a business structure: a sole proprietorship, partnership, or corporation.

- File the forms necessary to establish your business structure.

- Apply for a local and/or state business license (for local licenses, contact county government; for state licenses, apply at the secretary of state's office or online at your state's Web site).

- Check zoning laws and adhere to them.

- Make sure you follow any and all laws, rules, regulations, guidelines, and policies.

Sole proprietorship

In a sole proprietorship, the owner and the business are considered a single entity. The owner is liable for all business debts, and also is at the greatest risk. As sole proprietor, you have the right to transfer all or part of the business, and you can report profits or losses from the business on your personal income tax returns. The sole proprietor has complete control of the operation of the business and makes all business decisions without consulting anyone else. This business structure is considered informal in some states and requires little paperwork. If you are on your own when you first start out, this is probably your best option. If you decide later that you would like to have a partner, you can always change it then. If the business is in your name, then it usually does not require any registration at any level of government. If the business is in another name (for example,

Mountainside Medical Billing), then you will need to file a "doing business as" (DBA) form.

Business ownership has appealed to many people over the years for many different reasons. The ultimate freedom in the work world is being your own boss because there is no reporting to supervisors and no one looking over your shoulder to evaluate your performance and critique your work quality. You will have the ultimate say on all business decisions related to your medical billing company; you never again have to hold back your ideas and opinions when you know there is a better way of doing things. If you are considering owning and operating a medical billing company from home, you will have unlimited flexibility with your time and schedule. Much of the work medical billing requires can be done either day or night. Whether you are an early riser or a night owl, access to your computer is all you need. This flexibility is extremely valuable to parents or other caregivers, people who are working more than one job, or those who have circumstances that limit their ability to commute to the workplace. Parents of school-age children can begin working when their children leave in the morning and stop working when they come home. Parents who have children at home during the day can work at night while the children sleep.

Partnership

A partnership is also considered an informal business structure. It is similar to a sole proprietorship but has two or more owners. Each partner is liable for his or her portion of the business, and debts, profits, and losses are shared proportionately among the partners. As with the sole proprietorship, partners may report profits and losses on their personal income tax returns; however, an informational return must be filed, listing the partnership's profits or losses. If you and someone else decide on a partnership, you should draw up a written agreement specifically outlining each partner's duties, responsibilities, liabilities, and rights. Determine how profits will be shared, how decisions will be made and disputes resolved, and how the partnership will be dissolved or bought out if needed. A formal partnership agreement drawn up by a lawyer can help avert problems in case the partnership dissolves.

One key difference between a partnership and a sole proprietorship is that the business does not cease to exist with the death of a partner. Under such circumstances, the deceased partner's share can either be taken over by a new partner, or the partnership can be reorganized to accommodate the change. In either case, the business is able to continue without much disruption.

Although not all entrepreneurs benefit from turning their sole proprietorship businesses into partnerships, some thrive when incorporating partners into the business. In such instances, the business benefits significantly from the knowledge and expertise each partner contributes toward the overall operation of the business. As your business grows, it may be advantageous for you to come together in a partnership with someone who is knowledgeable about medical billing or management and will be able to contribute toward the expansion of the operation. Sometimes as a sole proprietorship grows, the needs of the company outgrow the knowledge and capabilities of the single owner, requiring the input of someone who has the knowledge and experience necessary to take the company to its next level.

Limited Liability Company (LLC)

A Limited Liability Company (LLC), often wrongly referred to as limited liability corporation, is not quite a corporation, yet is much more than a partnership. An LLC encompasses features found in the legal structure of corporations and partnerships, which allows the owners — called "members" in the case of an LLC — to enjoy the same liability protection of a corporation and the record-keeping flexibility of a partnership, like not having to keep meeting minutes or records. In an LLC, the members are not personally liable for the debts incurred for and by the company, and profits can be distributed as deemed appropriate by its members. In addition, all expenses, losses, and profits of the company flow through the business to each member, who would ultimately pay either business taxes or personal taxes — and not both on the same income.

An LLC type of business organization would be most appropriate for a business that is not quite large enough to warrant assuming the expenses incurred in becoming a corporation or being responsible for the record-keeping involved in operating as such. But yet, the extent of its operations requires a better legal and financial shelter for its members.

Regulations and procedures affecting the formation of LLCs differ from state to state, and they can be found on the Internet in your state's "corporations" section of the secretary of state office Web site. There are two main documents that are normally filed when establishing an LLC. One is an operating agreement, which addresses issues such as the management and structure of the business, the distribution of profit and loss, the method of how members will vote, and how changes in the organizational structure will be handled. The operating agreement is not required by every state.

The second document that is filed when starting an LLC is the articles of organization, which is required by every state, and the required form is generally available for download from your state's Web site. The purpose of the articles of organization is to legally establish your business by registering with your state. It must contain, at a minimum, the following information:

- The LLC's name and the address of the principal place of business

- The purpose of the LLC

- The name and address of the LLC's registered agent (the person who is authorized to physically accept delivery of legal documents for the company)

- The name of the manager or managing members of the company

- An effective date for the company and signature

Corporation

Corporations are the most formal type of all the legal business structures discussed so far. A corporation can be established as a public or a private corporation. A public corporation is owned by its shareholders (also known as stockholders) and is public because anyone can buy stocks in the company through public stock exchanges. Shareholders are owners of the corporation through the ownership of shares or stocks that represent a financial interest in the company. Not all corporations start up as corporations, selling shares in the open market. They may actually start up as individually owned businesses that grow to the point where selling its stocks in the open market is the most financially feasible business move for the organization. However, openly trading your company's shares diminishes your control over it by spreading the decision-making abilities to stockholders or shareholders and a board of directors. Some of the most familiar household names, like Tupperware Corporation and The Sports Authority, Inc., are public corporations.

A private corporation is owned and managed by a few individuals who are normally involved in the day-to-day decision-making and operations of the company. If you own a relatively small business but still wish to run it as a corporation, a private corporation legal structure would be the most beneficial form for you as a business owner because it allows you to stay closely involved in the operation and management. Even as your business grows, you can continue to operate as a private corporation. There are no rules for having to change over to a public corporation once your business reaches certain size. The key is in the retention of your ability to closely manage and operate the corporation. For instance, some of the large companies that we are familiar with and tend to assume are public corporations happen to be private corporations — companies such as L.L. Bean and Mary Kay Cosmetics.

Whether private or public, a corporation is its own legal entity capable of entering into binding contracts and being held directly liable in any legal issues. Its finances are not directly tied to anyone's personal finances, and taxes are addressed completely separately from its owners. These are only some of the many advantages to operating your medical billing business in the form of a corporation. However, forming a corporation is no easy task, and not all business operations lend themselves to this type of setup. The process can be lengthy and put a strain on your budget due to all the legwork and legal paperwork involved. In addition to the start-up costs, there are additional ongoing maintenance costs, as well as legal and financial reporting requirements not found in partnerships or sole proprietorships.

To legally establish your corporation, it must be registered with the state in which the business is created by filing articles of incorporation. Filing fees, information to be included, and the format of the articles of incorporation vary from state to state. However, some of the information most commonly required by states is listed as follows:

- Name of the corporation

- Address of the registered office

- Purpose of the corporation

- Duration of the corporation

- Number of shares the corporation will issue

- Duties of the board of directors

- Status of the shareholders, such as quantity of shares and responsibilities

- Stipulation for the dissolution of the corporation

- Names of the incorporator(s) of the organization

- Statement attesting to the accuracy of the information contained therein

- Signature line and date

S Corporation

An S Corporation is a form of legal structure, under IRS regulations, designed for the small businesses — "S Corporation" meaning Small Business Corporation. Operating under S Corporation means the company is taxed closely to how a partnership or sole proprietor would be taxed, rather than being taxed like a corporation.

Operating under the S Corporation legal structure, the shareholders' taxes are directly affected by the business's profit or loss. Any profits or losses the company may experience in any one year are passed through to the shareholders who in turn must report them as part of their own income tax returns. According to the IRS, shareholders must pay taxes on the profits the business realized for that year in proportion to the stock they own.

In order to organize as an S Corporation and qualify as such under the IRS regulations, the following requirements must be met:

- It cannot have more than 100 shareholders.

- Shareholders must be U.S. citizens or residents.

- It must be able to meet the requirements for an S Corporation the entire year.

Additionally, Form 2553, "election of Small Business Corporation," must be filed with the IRS within the first 75 days of the corporation's fiscal year.

Electing to operate under S Corporation status is not effective for every business; however, it has proved to be beneficial for a number of companies through many years of operation. Because of the significant role S Corporations play in the U.S. economy, S-Corp., the S-Corporation Association of America, was established in 1996 to serve as a lobbying force in Washington, protecting the small and family-owned businesses from too much taxation and government mandates. Membership in the association comprises S Corporations both big and small from throughout the nation.

Making a Commitment

Starting a new medical billing business should be one of the most important decisions you make in your life, and commitment is crucial when it comes to helping your business succeed. Starting a new business will not be easy; you must be up for a challenge. Some days you will have a smooth day where everything goes well, and then there will be days where nothing goes well and you do not get anything done. Your own determination and commitment will keep your business on the right track, and there will be many important decisions to make along the journey of business ownership.

You should start thinking about whether to begin your medical billing business from home or to locate office space and work away from home. It is more financially feasible to begin working from home, provided you have the available workspace and technological capabilities. The start-up costs typically run at least $5,000 for a home-based business, and that amount can increase depending on your business needs. For a medical billing service, you will need the following essentials: a computer with printer, a telephone, fax machine, high-speed Internet access, and a second phone line for business purposes only. As your business grows, you may need to hire employees and move to an office space with more room. There are several aspects to consider when budgeting for this step, including rent, utilities, and rental insurance. It takes money to make money and a lot of committed time to build a successful business. The medical billing business can be an expensive business to start, but this does not have to be the case. There are several ways you can keep your costs down.

Working from home will help minimize start-up costs if you have a computer system that can handle the workload, or if you purchase a new computer as your first business expense. *More about business locations and equipment will be discussed in Chapter 8.*

Consider working part-time when starting off because it will take a while to build your clientele. Do not quit your regular job until you are making an amount that you are comfortable with, or at least an amount equal to your work salary.

If you will file claims electronically, it is done via the Internet, so be sure your Internet connection is fast and dependable. It is wise to choose a digital subscriber line (DSL) so when you need to get online, you will have instant access instead of having to dial up.

Software will be one of the biggest investments for your company, and you must research it thoroughly. You can look to spend anywhere from $400 to $6,000 for your software needs. You will need to invest in medical billing software, human resources software when you start hiring employees, and financial software to keep track of income and expenses. Word processing software, spreadsheets, and any other similar software is pretty basic and can be bought at a reasonable cost at a discount store, a business supply shop, or online. *Current available software is discussed in Chapter 4.*

Your business's first bills

After you have listed everything, you can add up all the costs. Once you start your medical billing business, there will still be monthly expenses that need to be paid, regardless of whether you earn income right away. Your monthly bills will more than likely double or triple if you have an office outside your home.

Expenses that you will be responsible for paying (whether your office is in your home or at another location) are as follows:

1. If you have a loan, then you will have a monthly loan payment.

2. Your Internet service will need to be paid monthly. Sometimes Internet service providers (ISPs) offer great discounts to customers who can pay for six or 12 months upfront or to new customers, so you might want to ask about this. Another decision to make is whether you want to combine Internet, phone, and fax lines into one bill, from the same provider (either your ISP, telephone company, or cable television service provider).

3. Office supplies: paper, printer ink, and so on.

4. Advertising and marketing materials.

5. Telephone service, paid monthly, that you can also use for a fax line, plus installation (unless you are using an existing home telephone service).

6. Postage and postage meter.

7. Utilities (gas, heat, air conditioning, electricity, sewage, trash pickup) need to be paid monthly.

8. Clearinghouse fees.

9. Claim submission fees (fees vary, but an average is around 50 cents for each claim submitted from the MIB to the clearinghouse).

10. Computer software.

The following chart is an example of a start-up cost sheet analysis that compares home office costs to costs for an external office. It will give you an idea of what to expect.

Sample budget sheet for start-up costs

	External office	Home office
Monthly rent	$800	$0
Office supplies	$7,000	$4,000
Insurance	$700	$600
CMS forms	$35	$35
Software	$500 (varies)	$500 (varies)
Utilities	$150	$0
Employees	Will vary	$0
Clearinghouse	$300	$300
Business license	$100	$100
Total estimate	$9,585	$5,535

The following chart is a sample start-up sheet you can fill in for your business, using the blank lines to add any additional items and their cost. Once you have looked over the sample budget sheet for start-up costs, you can see what expenses are involved. After you have filled it in, add it up to determine the costs of your start-up expenses. Leave space for unanticipated expenses — there are always a few surprises in any budget or estimate.

Business start-up costs sheet

Rent/security deposit* . . . .$_____

Business insurance . . . .$_____

Advertising/marketing. . . . . $_____

Telephone/utilities . . . .$_____

CMS 1500 forms (case of 2500) . . . . (usually about $25) $_____

Internet service . . . .$_____

Legal/lawyer/IRS fee (required to start, incorporate,

and license your business) . . . .$_____

Accounting . . . .$_____

Equipment . . . .$_____

Payroll . . . .$_____

Professional/business memberships . . . .$_____

Training/schooling/certification. . . . .$_____

_____ . . . .$_____

_____ . . . .$_____

_____ . . . .$_____

_____ . . . .$_____

_____ . . . .$_____

_____ . . . .$_____

_____ . . . .$_____

Total = ...$_____

*Make sure you add all your deposits of installations and
deposits of services, even when working with rent and utilities.*

Goal Setting

Everyone has a goal in life, and perhaps one of your goals is to own the most successful medical billing business in your state. What are your reasons for wanting to own and operate a medical billing business?

- Do you want to make more money?

- Do you like the medical field?

- Do you like the idea of owning your own business?

- Do you want to be your own boss?

- Do you work for a doctor now and do medical billing for him or her?

- Do you want to earn money while staying at home with your children?

Whatever your reasons are, you must set goals for your medical billing business's success. Start with short-term goals and eventually work your way up to long-term goals. Short-term goals can be as simple as making up brochures for your business, finding your first client, figuring out and setting up the location of your office, building a Web site, or naming your business. A long-term goal could be having a certain amount of clients within the first year, hiring employees, expanding your business into a larger office, or bringing in a business partner. Below are examples of short-term and long-term goals.

Short-term goals for your medical billing business might include:

- Locate an office.

- Equip your office with necessities, such as a computer, printer, fax, copier, and phone.

- Have office utilities turned on.

- Purchase insurance for your business.

- Find your first client.

- Get your first claim paid.

Long-term goals for your medical billing business might include:

- Find a larger office.

- Hire employees.

- Stay in business longer than three to five years (roughly half of small businesses fail in their first five years, according to the Small Business Administration).

- Achieve popularity.

- Achieve a certain number of clients.

- Become one of the largest medical billing businesses in the nation.

Above are examples; your goals can be whatever you choose. List your short-term and long-term goals, keep them nearby, and work on one goal at a time. Take your time and accomplish your goals in stride. Also keep in mind that it is normal for short- and long-term goals to change over time. Many medical billing company owners review their goals annually and change or add to them. Below are suggestions for goals you might want to pursue in regard to your new medical billing business:

- More income (specify a dollar amount if you want).

- More clients (be more specific if you want).

- Expand your business by providing other services to your clients.

- Move business from home to a separate office.

- Hire employees (or hire more of them).

- Find a lawyer.

- Hire an accountant.

Do not set yourself up for failure by writing down all these goals and leaving them unmarked for long periods of time. If you are determined to be successful, writing down and tracking your goals will keep you on course to meet these goals.

After you have picked a name for you business and decided which structure will best fit your operations, the next step is establishing your business plan. This plan will be the foundation for your business, so make it as detailed as possible.

Chapter 6

Establishing a Business Plan

Your business plan is a concise, yet comprehensive, summary of your medical billing services, your business strategy, your financial plan, and your mission within the industry you have chosen. It also includes your background, your experience, and how you propose to manage your staff. It serves as evidence to your investors that you have researched all aspects in making yourself completely knowledgeable of the business, and that you have prepared a realistic strategy for making your business succeed. *There is a sample business plan in Appendix A in the back of this book, as well as on the companion CD-ROM.* Use this example when you are writing a business plan for your medical billing business.

When you decide you want to open and run a new medical billing business, there must be some kind of business strategy to make it successful. When you are asking investors to come in and join you on your business journey, they will want to know every detail of your business strategy. When developing your business strategy into a business plan, you will want to make sure you include everything you possibly can about your business and the kind of short-term and long-term goals you would like to establish. You will need to submit a formal business plan to prospective funders/investors. You can write this yourself or hire someone to write it for you. Before writing your medical billing company's business plan, you need to define the plan's target audience clearly (for example, bank lending officer or potential investors); determine the plan's length; map out the business plan's structure; determine the plan's requirements in terms of levels of detail and the contents; and identify the main issues it will address.

An organized, logical, and concise business plan will help potential funders and investors better understand the business's structure, plans, and goals.

The following is the basic, yet most important, information to include in a business plan:

- Your business goals

- Ways you will accomplish those goals

- Potential problems you may encounter along the way and how you plan to handle them

- The organizational structure (as it is today and how you plan it to be in the future)

- The amount of capital you will need to get the business started and to keep it in operation

Beyond these five most important things to include in a business plan are the key sections that the business plan will include (and must include). The key sections of your medical billing company's business plan will be:

1. **Mission statement** — This should include the purpose of your business, the goods or services that you provide, and a statement as to your company's attitude towards your employees and customers

2. **Executive summary** – Summarizes the key points of the entire business plan

3. **Company description** — Provides information about the beginning of your company and its products and/or services

4. **Management** — Includes short biographies for management team members you have hired so far and a hiring plan for additional members of management and staff

5. **Market/industry analysis** — Provides industry background, target market, product description, and marketing approach strategies

6. **Customer analysis** — This describes who your business will serve

7. **Competitive analysis** — Lists and describes your top competitors

8. **Marketing strategy** — Describes your business products and services, pricing strategy, sales and distribution, advertising, and promotion

9. **Operations** — Describes internal functions and positions of the company

10. **Strengths and weaknesses** — Describes the particulars of your business that have enabled you to be successful, and those that will continue to enable you to be successful

11. **Financial projections** — Describes highlights of your financial statements

12. **Conclusion** — Highlights key issues discussed in the plan

13. **Supporting documents** — Includes your financial statements and other supporting documents referred to in your medical billing business plan

All business plans need to show actual or projected monthly cash flow — or both — for a minimum of 12 months. Your business plan should show how much money you are getting and where it comes from. You also need to show what your money is being spent on. The point to this is that positive cash flow pays bills, and businesses that cannot show positive cash flows do not pay their bills. A business plan should state your medical billing company's priorities, and it should also include specific business milestones (projects). Spending budgets and deadlines for these milestones should be included along with a list of employees responsible for achieving each one. This helps establish responsibility within the business and notes how each milestone will be measured and tracked.

A basic business plan should be no more than ten pages, plus appendices and financial statements. It will require more research than writing. There is no universal standard timeline for updating a business plan, but it should be reviewed and completely updated at least once a year.

A more comprehensive business plan is longer, and its purpose is to obtain a bank loan or to seek venture capital. A comprehensive business plan will probably run ten to 20 pages. The market analysis and financial projections will take the most time to research and write.

If the whole idea of writing a business financial plan is overwhelming, you can purchase a standardized, formatted business plan template online and fill in all the necessary details in a way that will still be professional and presentable. This option will cost less because you still have to do most of the work yourself. You can also purchase software that will help you develop a business plan step-by-step, like Business Plan Pro®, which has 500 sample plans.

A lot of Web sites provide steps, advice, and questions to consider when writing your business plan. You might want to read through some of these before beginning to write yours (find them by doing an online search of writing a business plan). Consider hiring a professional business start-up consultant to review your business plan from the investor's point of view, but expect to pay a decent amount for this service.

SCORE, a national organization committed to assisting small businesses, has business plan templates available online for free at **www.score.org/ template_gallery.html**. Also available are templates for a balance sheet, bank loan request, cash flow statement, financial forecast, profit and loss projections, sales forecasts, and start-up expenses.

There are a number of other Web sites that provide you with a variety of samples and templates that can also be used as reference, such as **www.**

bplans.com, **www.nebs.com/nebsEcat/business_tools/bptemplate**, and **www.planmagic.com**.

Drafting Your Business Plan

The first page of your business plan will be your cover page. The cover page should include the company name in all-capital letters (then skip a few lines), "Business Plan" centered on the page, followed (after a couple line spaces) by the company's address, contact name (your name), and current date. After your cover page, you will want to include your table of contents.

Sample cover page

**Name of Company
Business Plan**

Address
Contact Name
Date

Table of Contents

I.   Mission Statement
II.   Executive Summary
III. Description of Proposed Business
IV.   Management and Staffing
V.   Market/Industry Analysis
      a. Industry background
      b. Target market
      c. Product description
      d. Market approach strategy
VI.   Marketing Strategy
VII. Operations
VIII. Strengths and Weaknesses
IX.   Financial Projections
X.   Conclusion
XI.   Supporting Documents

Mission statement

Your mission statement is your opportunity to communicate the goal and vision of your medical billing company. It is important to illustrate what sets you apart from the competition because everyone will promise to provide good service. Use language that conveys your purpose and how your business will serve the needs of your market. Take the time to work on your mission statement until it meets your satisfaction because you will be using it in your advertising materials and on your Web site, as well as other business documentation. You can also look at it as your promise to your clients. A mission statement should state what the business's goals are and what the company promises to do. It does not need to be long. Often, a short mission statement conveys its message the best. Below is an example of a medical billing company's mission statement:

Star Medical Billing Services is dedicated to your success as a health care provider by providing you with efficient and high-quality electronic medical insurance billing solutions and services.

If you sit down and think about your mission statement, you will want to honestly think about why your clients would want to come to you. Most clients want someone whom they can trust and who does not ignore their phone calls. They also want someone who will give them immediate attention and take their account seriously, as if it were the only one the medical biller had. Clients would choose a medical biller who, if he or she happens to see an error on their day sheet, would not hesitate to let the physician know. If a client knew something that should be changed about the medical billing practice, the MIB should welcome the advice. Clients want an MIB who is willing to help their practice succeed, along with the medical billing business.

Executive summary

Your executive summary should take all the key points from your medical billing business plan and present them in a clear, concise format. It needs to state the services your company will offer, the need for services in terms of the industry's current trends, the market you are hoping to reach, and the financial plan for your business. The executive summary should be compelling — you hope to convince your investors that this is a business that will be successful and profitable. It should only be one or two pages, and it should be written last because it will be a summary of the information presented in your business plan.

Description of business

This section is where you will describe in detail the purpose of the business plan. State what your business intends to accomplish. Describe your goods, services, and the role your business will play in the overall global market. Explain what makes your business different than all of its competitors, and clearly identify your business's goals and objectives. The business description section should number one to two pages in length.

Management and staffing

Management describes you, your skills, background, and industry knowledge and experience. All of your education, training, licenses, certifications, and relevant work experience have helped prepare you to own and operate a medical billing business. The management and staffing section of your business plan could be as short as one paragraph if you are the only employee, or it could be as long as two pages, depending on the number of employees you have or plan to hire. Identifying your management team's names and positions, along with other staff members and their jobs, will show that your business will be well-run and well-managed. As that old saying goes, a company's greatest asset is its employees. Also be sure to identify positions that you may need to fill in the future in order to expand your business.

Market/industry analysis

The market/industry analysis section should demonstrate your knowledge of the medical billing business. Do your research and include information that you have acquired through data collection and research. Many sources of information are available, online and through printed media. The research and findings will make your presentation valid and you will be better prepared to answer questions that arise. In your market/industry analysis, be sure to include a general description of the medical billing industry, description and needs of your targeted customer, a description of your services, identification of your competition, and your planned strategy and approach. The market/industry analysis should be one of the most thorough sections of the business plan, and it can be several pages long. The target market section of this analysis requires a little more focus.

The target market section is one of the largest sections of the business plan because you will be addressing key issues that will determine the volume of sales and revenue that you will be able to generate for your business. The target market is who your customer, or groups of customers, will be. Identify the characteristics of the principal market you intend to target, such as demographics, market trends, and geographic location.

Marketing strategy

The marketing strategy element of the business plan will identify current and potential customers, along with the methods you will use to advertise your medical billing business to them. The marketing strategy portion of your business plan is likely to be at least three to four pages long, depending on the amount of detail you include. The marketing strategy section should include the following: products and services, pricing strategy, sales and distribution plan, and advertising and promotions plan.

Operations

All aspects of your medical billing business's management and services will be discussed in the operations section of your business plan. Focus your discussion on how to improve your business operation resources, which will advance your business's success. All of the information outlined in this section needs to be backed by realistic numbers, such as the cost of renting an office, the cost of purchasing or leasing office equipment, salaries, utilities, and so on.

Discuss your medical billing business's current location in detail. If you have employees, or anticipate hiring employees, describe briefly the tasks they will perform.

Strengths and weaknesses

In this section of your business plan, detail the particular aspects of your business that have enabled you, and will continue to enable you, to be successful. Describe the factors that give you an advantage over your competitors; maybe it will be your medical billing work experience, or the certifications you and your employees hold.

Addressing any particular weaknesses will help you to overcome them or deal with them better. Your competitors have weaknesses also, so your business is not the only one that has to overcome them. Some of your business's weaknesses may be inexperience and limited exposure to the market, both of which you can overcome with time and experience. Some weaknesses, however, cannot be overcome and must be dealt with head on. You must identify these factors and detail how you plan to take on each one. Keep this section fairly short — no more than a single page.

Financial projections

Because you are just starting up your medical billing business, working with estimates based on similar businesses' performances will be acceptable. If you are using the business plan as part of the application process for a loan, then be sure to match your financial projections to the requested loan amount.

When you are developing your medical billing business's financial projections, you must take into consideration every single possible expense, expected and unexpected, and still be conservative in your revenues. It is not essential that your actual revenues exceed the estimated amount, but it is not a good situation when expenses are more than expected. Your projections should be addressed for the next three to five years, breaking down each year with the following information: forecasted income statements, cash flow statements, balance sheets, and capital expenditure budgets. This section will most likely make up several pages of your business plan, and you might want to include some graphs along with the budget forms to show the information more clearly.

Conclusion

The conclusion is the last written part of your business plan. Use this part to highlight key issues discussed in each section, and then conclude the business plan here with a summary of your future plans for the progress of your business. Use language that will help the reader see what you will be able to accomplish and how successful your business will be if it receives the support you are requesting.

Supporting documents

Your business plan will certainly be strengthened and considered more valuable with attached supporting documentation, but do not include too many attachments or readers will be overwhelmed. Ask yourself if each particular document will make a difference; if not, then leave it out. Documents that you will most likely want to attach include:

- Copies of the business principals' résumés

- Tax returns and personal financial statements of the principals for the last three years

- A copy of licenses, certifications, and other relevant legal documents

- A copy of the lease or purchase agreement, if you are leasing or buying space

Creating Your Business's Financial Plan

Every business must have a carefully thought-out and written financial plan as part of its business plan. If you decide to apply for a bank loan, the bank will want to see your financial plan. The financial plan's strategy is to show the amount of funds needed to start your medical billing business, how you plan to use the money, and the timeline for the money. If you have one, your accountant or financial advisor will be very helpful in developing it by helping you outline the business's financial structure before you begin writing the business plan.

There is no universal rule for updating a business financial plan, but it should be updated on a regular basis. Some business owners prefer to update the financials quarterly to keep information up-to-date.

Your financial plan will include your medical billing company's start-up budget; its operations budget for the first year of business; and quarterly information for the next two years.

The first step of your medical billing company's financial plan will focus on the short-term (two or three years) or long-term (five years) financial statements, like income statement, balance sheet, and cash flow statement.

The second step is to take a look at start-up costs and itemize the costs before the company is launched to determine how much capital is needed. Sample start-up costs include insurance, lease payments, equipment, business license and registration, marketing, and salaries for employees. The start-up costs for each business will vary depending on where your business is located, what kind of business structure you use, whether you initially hire employees, and more.

Revenue projections are the third part of your business financial plan. What will drive revenues in your medical billing business's first years of operation? Develop revenue assumptions for the first five years of operation. Include staff salaries, and show their effect on business revenue.

Examining cash flow is the final step of a financial plan. Your business cash flow statement should always show a positive ending balance. If the cash flow is negative, then your company is underfunded and needs to raise additional capital in the start-up phase.

Ask yourself the following questions and include the answers in your medical billing business's financial plan:

- Where will I get start-up funds?

- How will I pay for my medical billing business until it starts to generate income?

- What happens if it takes a longer time to get clients than expected?

- How will I be able to keep cash flowing once I do have clients?

- How do I keep track of income and expenses and use cash flow wisely?

You must have a financially well-established back-up plan, at least until you have a roster of consistent, dependable clients. A back-up plan is a way to prevent chaos in times of business financial crisis. This plan needs to focus on cash flow and must consist of these important elements: workforce (you may have to be reduced during a crisis); equipment (you may have to sell or change it); headquarters (you may have to move it to a cheaper location to cut costs); and technology (your business might need to invest in new technology to cut its costs, but you must understand what you need and do not need). Your financial plan should consist of the following, but it is not limited to:

Start-up expenses

- Registration fees for business status (LLC, LP, LLP, corporation, S Corporation)

- Equipment

- Rent deposit

- Utility deposits and fees

- Software

- Memberships in medical billing industry organizations

Operating expenses

- Rent payment

- Utility payments

- Advertising

- Business loan payment

- Office equipment payment

- Claim submissions fees

You will want to fill out the following for your financial plan:

- Income statement

- Balance sheet

- Projected cash flow sheet

After you have written your business plan, you will be able to use this document to approach investors, or even family or friends, to see if they would be willing to help finance your new business. You will also need this document if you decide to approach a bank or other lending institution to fund your new venture. The next chapter focuses on financing your business, the next logical step to implement after developing a business plan.

Chapter 7

Financing Your New Business

This section will address the financing of your medical billing business. To start your business, you must have funds to pay business-related expenses and meet payroll costs. A business loan can help you pay for the equipment, software, and supplies you will need.

It is difficult to find the funds to manage all the costs involved in starting up your business. If you are considered high-risk, you will have a hard time getting a loan because the bank will feel you are too much of a liability and might have difficulty repaying a loan. People with a heavy debt load, bad credit, poor credit history, late or missed payments, little or no collateral, or little or no credit are considered high risk. Make sure you will be able to pay back any money that you borrow for your medical billing business, and make sure the payments will fit in your budget until the business is self-sustaining. You can also try to keep your costs down when starting by financing your business yourself.

There are many ways to get the funds for starting up. Your options consist of, but are not limited to:

- Personal savings and/or certificates of deposit (CDs)

- Credit cards

- Bank loans

- Small Business Association loans

- Other business loan sources

- Private loans from investors

- Family/friends

- Equity investments

- Home equity loan

Use this information as a starting point to figure out which route is best for you to take. If you are serious about starting a medical billing business, come up with a sound financial plan, see who would be interested in investing, and invite these individuals to a meeting. Let them know you want to open a medical billing business, show them the research you have done, explain how much it should cost to open it, and see if they would like to help. When taking this route, you will need to have a business plan already written and finalized because any potential investors will want to see this important document. If you do a presentation for your friends, family, potential investors, and partners, and they see how determined you are and how much of a need there is for medical billing, they may be interested. But you need to put an effective presentation together and prove to them investing in your business would be a wise thing to do.

This next section will cover all the ways you can obtain funding for your medical billing business. One of the first places you should consider looking is in your own bank account.

Personal Savings and Certificates of Deposit (CDs)

No specific amount of money is required or advised, but of course, the more money you have saved up to help start your business, the better off you will be because you will not need to borrow as much. If you have any personal CDs, you may want to consider cashing those in to provide funding for your business. In addition to the actual start-up costs, you will need to consider that it might be several months before your medical billing business starts turning a profit. If you are employed with a current job, it might be a good idea to do medical billing part-time and keep your job while you are establishing your business; you can run your medical billing business full-time once you have a long-term commitment from at least one or two investors.

Personal savings and CDs will also come in handy should you decide to borrow money to establish your new business. You will need to repay any loans you take out; having some savings set aside will help you stay on top of your finances while you are waiting for your business to start making a profit.

Credit Cards

If you do not have substantial savings to invest or if you have difficulty obtaining a loan, you can use a credit card for some of your purchases. Credit card limits are based on your credit and, if you have excellent credit, you will more than likely be able to obtain an approved line of credit for business use. If you have poor credit, then you will not be approved or be able to get a credit card. Just as with any loan, you will be responsible for paying a monthly payment on all credit cards, most likely with an interest rate higher than you would receive with a bank loan. This method can be an expensive way to finance your new business, but if you have no other options and are determined to start a business, opening a credit card might be your answer.

Obtaining a Loan to Finance Your Business

When you approach a bank or credit union to request a loan to start up your medical billing business, you will have to state your need clearly and provide all the required supporting financial documentation. A loan proposal is the most professional way to present your request.

It will also be important to have most of the legal requirements of your medical billing business completed before you start to apply for financing for start-up funds or a loan. You will need to supply your EIN and personal identification information about the business owner(s), including name, address, social security number (SSN), and photo identification. This will be run through the Office of Foreign Assets Control (OFAC), which checks the information against outstanding arrest warrants. Your SSN will also be run through a credit check. All the information is necessary since the advent of the USA Patriot Act (Uniting and Strengthening America by Providing Appropriate Tools Required to Intercept and Obstruct Terrorism Act of 2001), which increases the ability of law enforcement agencies to search telephone, e-mail communications, medical, financial, and other records.

A loan proposal is practically a condensed version of your business plan because you will want to provide the bank with enough information for them to make an informed decision about loaning you the money. The financial information you provide must be brief, yet present a full picture of your business, containing all the critical information they will need. The loan proposal you prepare must be a professional document with timely and accurate information about your business, including any possible future changes in the company.

Try to be conservative in developing your revenue estimates for the financial projections of your business loan proposal because very high revenues may be assumed to be unrealistic. When estimating expenses, consider all possible costs and be sure to avoid underestimating expenses, because it is better to overestimate your costs and end up having excess funds than to underestimate your expenses and wind up needing money for business necessities. It is considered good practice to include a description of how you arrived at your revenue and expenses figures.

A solid business loan proposal will include a written account of the fundamental reasons you are seeking a loan, pertinent financial information, and all supporting documentation. Each bank may have different requirements for business loan applicants for a loan.

If you are unsure as to how much information you should provide in any one section of your business loan proposal, remember that there is no right or wrong way to do it. You just need to include what you feel is necessary to deliver your point to the loan officers.

Your medical billing business loan proposal will include:

- **General information** — Show the name of your business, name of the owners, owner's social security number or EIN, and business address.

- **Loan information** — State the purpose of your loan, the exact amount of funds requested, the requested terms of the loan (meaning length and interest rate), collateral you will use to secure the loan (include current market values), and how much equity you will be contributing to this business.

- **Business description** — Include the history and nature of the business, the business' legal structure, and an explanation of any future plans for the business and how the loan will benefit the business.

- **Market information** — Define the services your company provides, explain your business' market, and state your target customer base. Demonstrate that there is a demand for your services; identify your competitors and explain how you are able to compete in the global marketplace, and identify your customers and how you are able to serve them. Lastly, discuss your marketing plan and identify costs associated with it.

- **Business financial information** — Show your ability to pay the loan through financial projections. If this proposal is for a start-up loan, you will need to provide a projected balance sheet and income statement; for partnerships or sole proprietors, you will need to provide your and the other owners' financial statements.

- **Other supporting documentation** — Provide copies of important legal documents, such as articles of incorporation and DBA forms.

Now that you know the information you will need to provide to obtain a loan, consider the different types of loans available to you to finance your new medical billing business. One of the most popular places new business owners look for funding is the bank.

Bank loans

Sometimes it is difficult to obtain a bank loan to open a business if it is your first time as a small business owner. Your best bet is to seek out smaller banks that need your business and can be more accommodating. Try your personal bank first, and ask what kinds of business loans are available there. Most banks will expect to see a copy of your business plan. If you have collateral and a solid credit history, then you will more than likely be approved. If you are turned down, ask how you might make your application stronger before you apply to another bank.

You will also need to provide information on how the business is structured and any information about partnerships and corporations. If you are incorporated, the bank will want to see the by-laws and any association papers for your business. It will review personal financial statements of all major stakeholders, partners, or owners of the business. You will need to submit information on the purpose of your business, which you have already detailed in your business plan. The bank will make a decision on the approval of your loan based on the purpose of your business and what you are specifically seeking the loan for. For instance, you may need money to purchase real estate for your office. In this case, the bank will use the real estate as collateral on your loan. This is done the same way for equipment purchases, such as computers, software packages, and other equipment you may purchase for your business. The bank may ask you to sign a guarantee, which would ensure the repayment of the loan in the event that the business would fail. You will need to repay your loan back in monthly installments, depending on what you and your bank agreed on. If you provide everything requested and you have decent credit, you have a good possibility of receiving a loan, which will need to be repaid. If your business does not take off as quickly as you would like, make sure you have some way of paying back your bank loans and keeping up with those payments so you do not overextend your finances and default (get behind) on your loans.

Below are two banks that may be able to offer you funding. Remember, there are more options available to you than what is listed here, so do your research thoroughly before deciding on a lending institution. Your local bank may provide a better option than either of these large-scale institutions.

Bank of America™ (**www.bankofamerica.com/small_business/business_financing**) offers business lines of credit, business loans, SBA financing, and business leases (you can borrow the entire lease price of a new vehicle or equipment for your business). Business lines of credit include a business credit card or a Premium CreditLine. The business credit card is a way to control business expenses and/or finance your business accounts receivable. Obtain up to $25,000 credit at competitive rates, unsecured (not backed by collateral; has a higher interest rate than a secured loan), with variable monthly payments and revolving term lengths. You can draw funds as needed. A Premium CreditLine is a way to get working capital for your business or refinance debt, with no loan-closing costs and easy access to funds.

Wells Fargo® (**www.wellsfargo.com/biz**) offers business lines of credit as well as small business loans. Business lines of credit are flexible and enable business owners to repay and reuse their line of credit as needed. Business term loans enable owners to infuse their small business with immediate cash for long-term financing.

The business loans Wells Fargo offers vary by type, and some are secured by real estate. Two that are strictly business loans, with no real estate required to secure them, are the Wells Fargo BusinessLoan® term loan and the Equipment Express Loan. The BusinessLoan® term loan is unsecured at a fixed rate with flexible repayment terms. It is issued in a lump sum for long-term business financing from $10,000 to $100,000. The Equipment Express® Loan is a secured term loan for vehicle and equipment purchasing. It is a pre-approved credit amount with flexible terms and a fixed rate from $10,000 to $100,000.

Wells Fargo also offers secured (one in which an asset such as property is used as collateral to guarantee the loan) SBA loans from $5,000 to $5.2 million. The bank additionally provides checking accounts, savings accounts, and bill paying services to businesses, as well as financial management software and online invoicing through Wells Fargo Business Online.

Small Business Association loans

The SBA Web site (**www.sba.gov/financing**) provides assistance to small businesses and offers a variety of programs. The SBA also offers free online courses to help educate about small business ownership and financing.

Business owners may be able to borrow up to 100 percent of their financing needs from the SBA; however, the SBA usually prefers to loan more than just a few thousand dollars. The SBA can also offer longer financing terms with different payment options.

The SBA offers a Basic 7(a) Loan Program, which is actually provided by lenders who partner with the SBA. Most U.S. banks work with the SBA to provide loans to small business owners. Basic 7(a) Loans are available on a guaranty basis, which means loans are provided by lenders who structure their loans according to SBA's requirements, and apply and receive a guaranty from the SBA on a portion of each loan. SBA shares the loan risk with the lender (the risk that the borrower may not be able to pay back the loan in full), which means that it does not fully guaranty 7(a) loans.

The business owner applies to a lender (a bank or credit union) for financing for the loan, and the lender will decide if it will make the loan internally or if the application has weaknesses that will require the lender to obtain an SBA guaranty. The loan actually comes from a commercial lender, not from the government. The SBA cannot force a lender to provide a loan if it does not want to take the risk of doing so. SBA has no money to lend, so it cannot make loans. The loan applicant must be creditworthy and eligible for a bank loan.

All businesses considered for financing under the SBA 7(a) Loan Program must meet SBA size standards: be for-profit; be able to demonstrate repayment; and not already have personal or business resources to provide financing.

Important considerations for an SBA loan are:

- Collateral (personal)
- Management capability (the SBA and banks want to ensure whomever they lend money to will handle the funds responsibly and can make the business succeed)
- Owner's equity and contribution
- Size of loan
- Type of business
- How loan funds will be used
- Availability of funds from other sources

Other business loans

A few other potential business loan sources are listed below. Check these sites and see if any of these sources might be able to provide you with a small business loan at an affordable interest rate. Make sure you read, research, and check the fine print before you sign and agree to anything.

iBank[SM], **(www.ibank.com/small-business-loans.cfm?pbonav=loanty pes)**, enables companies of all sizes to store and organize business data for the purpose of arranging financing. iBank offers multiple loan programs and makes your single application available to multiple lenders for fast, direct funding. It also provides SBA loans. The many loan categories available at iBank include:

- Accounts receivable financing

- Bridge loans (short-term loans of two weeks to three years that are made pending the arrangement of a larger loan or a longer-term one)

- Business credit card

- Hard money loan (last resort loan; asset-based loan financing through which a borrower receives funds that are secured by the value of property; these loans usually have a much higher interest rate than a conventional loan)

- Lines of credit

- A retail/merchant cash advance (business owner receives a cash advance, no more than $150,000, quickly and without the paperwork required by banks; fee is at least 25 percent of the amount advanced)

- An unsecured business loan

- A working capital loan (to finance a company's everyday operations)

Yahoo!™ Small Business Loans Guide will help you learn more about the business loan process, the different types of loans, how to improve your chances for a loan, and much more (**http://smallbusiness.yahoo.com/r-article-a-2014-m-1-sc-10-business_loans_buyers_guide-i**). When considering what type of loan to apply for, it is a good place to start.

Private loans from investors and/or partners

You can put word out that you want to open a medical billing business and are looking for investors. Someone whom you know may know of someone wanting to invest his or her money in a new business venture. Someone who owns interest in a medical billing service already may be interested in investing in another one like yours. However, your lenders may feel they have the right to guide you in how you manage your business or may expect to be a part of the decision-making process. To avoid any future complications, have a lawyer present to validate the loan is a professional agreement, and make it clear you fully intend to repay it by a certain date. The lawyer can also draw up a formal and legal statement of the investors' rights regarding your business, and how much or how little they can or will be expected to be involved in making business decisions.

Loans from family and friends

The advantage to borrowing money from friends and family is the terms can be negotiated privately. Many friends or family members may not charge interest for the loan. The downside is sometimes it can be risky to mix personal and professional interests. You can ask your family to help you get your business off the ground; they can either provide their funding as a gift to help you start your new business venture, or they can give you a personal loan. Asking a family member or a friend can be a hard decision because if you borrow from them, they may act or think that they have a say in your business. Some family or friends may be pleased to help, while others will not be so pleased. You will need to put a sales pitch together so your family and friends will understand what you are doing, how you will succeed, and why you are opening your own business. Show them your business plan, goals, and financial expectations. You must make it worth their time and money to listen to your business proposal.

Equity Investments

There are different types of equity investments, which are investments where people are stockholders and invest in your business. Equity investments include the following:

- Venture capital

- Growth capital

- Leveraged buyout (LBO)

When funds are available for small businesses with great growth potential, or when funds are invested in these businesses, the funds are called **venture capital**. An investor is taking a chance on your business being potentially profitable, even though there is always the possibility of loss. Entrepreneurs must be able to demonstrate their business will be profitable in order to secure funding from investors.

Growth capital is a type of private equity investment. It is flexible and usually is a minor investment in a company that is seeking capital funds to expand, enter new markets, or finance an acquisition. Growth capital can also be used to help restructure a company's balance sheet.

An **LBO** is the acquisition of another company using a significant amount of borrowed money. The purpose of the LBO is to enable companies to make large acquisitions without committing a large amount of capital. Leverage can be created through futures, options, margins, and other financial instruments, and debt is used by most companies to finance their operations. Both the investor and the company benefit from leverage.

The different types of equity investments are for people who would like to help start up a company and help with the growth of operations. When you find someone who would like to invest in your medical billing company, decide which is the best option for both of you after considering your assets, expenses, and affordable financing choices. There are many investment options, but you and the investor will have to figure out what would better suit your business and both of you.

Home Equity Loan

A home equity loan is when the borrower uses the equity in his or her home as the loan collateral. A home equity loan or line of credit creates a lien (a legal claim on a property to obtain repayment for a debt) against the borrower's house and reduces the home's equity, or value. If a home equity loan is not paid, the bank can seize the home because it is the collateral for the loan. A business owner might seek a home equity loan in order to secure a loan for developing or growing his or her business. Home equity loans, sometimes referred to as second mortgages, are usually for a shorter term than first mortgages (usually around 15 years). They can be a business deduction on your business taxes; check with your accountant on this matter. A home equity loan is a one-time, lump-sum loan, usually with a fixed interest rate. The maximum amount of a home equity loan is determined by the borrower's income, credit history, and the home's value. Some states limit the amount people can borrow against their home, while some allow people to borrow 100 percent or even more of their home's equity. Your lender will know your state's laws. Generally, the maximum home equity loan is 75 percent or 80 percent of the home's appraised value.

A home equity line of credit is a revolving credit line, usually on a 20- or 30-year loan term, with an adjustable interest rate. Once approved for a home equity line of credit, the borrower can withdraw funds as needed. A home equity line of credit is also usually tax-deductible, especially when used to finance business operations.

According to the Federal Deposit Insurance Corporation (FDIC), an agency created by Congress to maintain stability and public confidence in the nation's financial system, people who get a home equity loan and then cannot make the payments on it will be subject to the lender foreclosing, causing them to lose their home. The FDIC recommends contacting several lenders to compare interest rates and terms on home equity loans and making sure you will be able to afford the monthly payments.

An online loan and mortgage site that lets people compare home equity loan rates is **www.mortgageloan.com.** This site allows you read information about a home equity loan versus a home equity line of credit. The site also has a home equity calculator, which can be very useful in helping you figure out how much you can afford to borrow and repay. Enter a loan amount, the term (number of years), and the interest rate, and it will calculate your monthly payment.

Once your new business has secure funding and a budget, you are ready to read the next chapter on finding the perfect location for your medical billing service. After deciding on a location for your business, you will need to pay for utilities, rent, equipment, and everything else you need to launch your business.

Chapter 8

New Business Basics

Will you work at home or will you work in an office away from home? This is one of the first decisions you must make after you secure financing for you new medical billing business. If you decide to locate an office away from home, it will be more challenging than making a place in your home for an office.

Work from a Home Office

Being in your own home has many incentives, such as waking up when you feel like it, going to work in your pajamas and slippers, and not being rushed. And because you will not be commuting, you will also save money on gas, which is one of the best aspects about working from home. A home office space can be located anywhere in your home where you can put your desk, computer, and a filing cabinet or two. You do not want a cramped place, but you do not need a large-capacity area, either. According to the Internal Revenue Service (IRS), in order to claim a business deduction for home office use, any area of your home designated as a home office needs to be used "exclusively and regularly as your principal place of business" (see Publication 587, "Business Use of Your Home," available at **www.irs.gov**).

A separate room is best for an office to have an official place of business and to have a place to keep everything related to your business. Working at home also gives you a tax break, and the IRS will allow you to write off some of your expenses from your home business. An accountant can help you put together your taxes, keep your records straight, and ensure you follow the law.

Working from home has advantages as well as disadvantages. Here are some pros and cons related to working from home:

Highlights of working from home:

- Not having to deal with high gas prices; you have everything you need in your home office

- If you have children, especially little ones who do not go to school yet, you will not have to worry about finding or paying a full-time babysitter (although you may need a sitter for a few hours a day if you find that you cannot get any work done)

- Electric, phone, water, and other utility bills should stay about the same

Drawbacks to working from home:

- Distractions, such as children, housework, and pets that need attention

- Cable TV can be a distraction for those who cannot resist turning on the television — and never get back to work

- Lack of social interaction (your days may get lonely without the day-to-day interaction of co-workers)

- Family members and friends may not consider working at home to be a "real" job

Some individuals choose this field of work because they have children at home, and if this is your case, you may have already made your decision. Working at home is a great idea because you are just starting out and you will not have to pay rent, renters' insurance, and taxes on any commercial property. However, working at home can unfortunately turn out to be a nightmare if you are not careful.

Do you have the self-discipline to screen calls from family members and friends, or not answer the door when you are working? This is an important factor to consider when deciding where to locate your business. It sometimes takes a while for people to realize you are working, even though you are at home. When they see you are committed to working from home and you have a regular work schedule, then they will be less likely to call you during your work hours. You might have to endure a few months of telling people that you will call them after you have finished working in order to set your work boundaries. Use your answering machine to screen calls — that is what it is for.

Of course, anyone who chooses to base his or her medical billing business at home needs to have the support of his or her spouse. Children will also learn to respect your work hours if you help them understand you are working. Many parents choose to work when their children are asleep, or when their spouse is home to take care of the kids. Other parents hire a sitter to come in and watch children in the morning or in the afternoon so they can work uninterrupted for a few hours.

While you may like the idea of being an MIB, ask yourself if you can handle it, as it is time-consuming, and you must be 100 percent committed. You should take a few years and build up your business; then, if you would like to expand with employees, at that point you should consider an outside office. Case study subjects in this book all seem to recommend this way of establishing your medical billing business in order to grow it slowly and steadily, and to minimize expenses these first few years while your business is getting established.

Work from an Office Away from Home

When looking for an office away from home, you must consider these details:

1. **How much will you spend on an office?** This includes monthly rent, utilities, and other costs that you would not incur in a home office. Depending on where your office is located, your monthly rent or mortgage payment may be extremely high.

2. **What type of parking will you need?** You will not have many clients coming to your office, as you will be the one going to see them. Make sure you have adequate parking for you, your employees (in the event your business expands and you hire employees), and the occasional visitor.

3. **How much office furniture will you need?** Spend your money wisely on desks, office chairs, bookcases, and filing cabinets. Then see what else you need in the way of furniture after you have opened and established your business. There is no need to buy everything upfront before you open your medical billing business.

Some of the advantages of working outside your home include:

- An office means business. There is no laundry or dirty dishes to distract you.

- You have the opportunity to interact with coworkers or clients on a regular basis and will not be as lonely.

Some disadvantages include:

- You will have to spend money on gas, nice clothes, lunches, and snacks.

- You will have a larger initial investment required to lease an office, buy office furniture and supplies, turn on utilities and telephone, and so on.

Your pets will be lonely without you at home to keep them company. When you start to look for office space, you can begin by consulting a real estate agent or simply by looking in your local newspaper's "For Rent" ads. If you have a specific neighborhood or area of town in mind, you may be able to find "Office Space for Rent" signs in vacant buildings. Because this is a business that does not cater to walk-in business, you do not need to seek a space that is easily accessible to foot traffic.

Locating your office in a medical office building could be helpful for networking and marketing purposes. However, rent in a medical complex is usually high, and this may not be the best choice if you have limited start-up funds.

A more economical option would be to lease a space in an office building or above a storefront. Make sure there is enough room for multiple workstations, depending on the number of employees you plan to eventually hire. Because your business depends on computer operations, you will need an office where the electric and phone lines are in perfect working order, with no faulty wiring or aging cables. You also might want to consider whether the building has wireless Internet capabilities. This could make accessing the Internet much easier, as you would not need someone to come and install special wiring every time you hire an employee; you would just have to pay for someone to establish your Internet connection.

Later, you may want to consider buying an office rather than renting, depending on how your business is going. In this case, consulting with a real estate agent who specializes in commercial properties will most likely save you time, energy, and money.

After you decide where to locate your business, the next expense you will have to consider is the utilities associated with your new business venture.

Utilities

When working from a home office or an office away from home, you will have the expense of utilities, which usually consist of electricity, water, gas, sewage, and possibly trash. The amount you will pay each month for utilities depends on where you live and from whom you rent (should you have an external office). Some landlords require their tenants to pay just the electric bill, while others require them to pay all utilities and related expenses. If you work from home, you will already have the expense of utilities, which may increase when you spend more hours at home working in your office. Utilities can become expensive and need to be taken into account when you are deciding where to locate your office, as it will definitely cost more money to heat and cool a 4,000-square-foot office away from home compared to a 400-square-foot home office.

Business Expenses

If you have a designated room that is set aside only for your office, you will most likely be able to deduct a portion of your utility bills on your business taxes, depending on what portion of your utilities is used solely for your business. If your home has ten rooms total, and one of those rooms is your home office, your accountant will be able to deduct one-tenth of your home's heating, cooling, and utility costs on your business taxes.

Any furnishings purchased for your home office are also tax-deductible because they are business expenses. The best way to determine if anything is completely tax-deductible is to save your receipts and give them to your accountant. Of course, any office equipment — like computers, printers, fax machines, and scanners — are all business expenses as well, and those receipts also need to be saved for your accountant.

Any work you have done to your home will indirectly affect your home office, so it might be deductible. Examples are replacement windows, exterior siding, carpet cleaning, new painting in your office, or any remodeling or new construction. Your accountant can best determine how this will affect your taxes in regard to business expenses and deductions.

Your Internet service provider's fee might be tax-deductible if most or all of your time online is for business. Again, you can set up a business account for your Internet service that would be separate from your home account so you can deduct the entire fee if it is appropriate. Ask your accountant.

Telephone expenses

A home office for any business should have its own phone number and answering machine to portray a dedicated business. If you choose to get a separate phone number and answering machine for your business, all those costs, including the monthly phone bills for that business number, should be deductible as business expenses. Some people may choose to use a cell phone for their business phone, and that is fine. Depending on how many personal calls you also get on that cell phone number, it may be questionable as fully tax-deductible because it is not a dedicated business line. Your accountant can clarify this for you, but to ensure a business deduction, you might be better off having a phone and answering machine set up in your office, with calls routed to your cell phone when you are out of the office and expecting business calls. This may entitle you to deduct business calls to and from your cell phone, or your monthly cell phone fee, as legitimate business expenses. Again, your accountant is the best advisor on these matters.

Business insurance

Insurance coverage is required to protect you, your medical billing business, and your employees. Business insurance is comparable to purchasing insurance to protect yourself, your car, and anyone else involved in case of an accident. You will need insurance for your office space whether you work away from home or in your home.

Several factors need to be considered when determining how much business rental insurance to purchase. General liability insurance coverage includes theft or damage to property and personal injury that may occur on business premises. If you employ more than four workers, state and federal laws will determine the minimum liability needed for personal injury and disease protection, which is workers' compensation. Business-interruption insurance (also called business income insurance) is also something you may want to consider in the event a fire or theft would make it impossible to continue to conduct business.

Even if you are working from home, purchasing business insurance is essential. Your homeowner's insurance will cover your equipment in the event of a loss, but will not cover loss of income if your business is interrupted. You will need to notify your homeowner's insurance provider (carrier) that you are running a business from your home to ensure your insurance plan will cover any accidents or mishaps that may occur there.

Another type of business insurance MIBs utilize is professional liability insurance. This offers financial protection if a client brings legal action against you or your business due to an error made in the provision of your services. "E&O," or "errors and omissions," insurance is another type of insurance you should have in case you are sued by someone who claims that your errors and omissions created a loss for them or their business.

Business insurance may be necessary if your business is located in commercial office space. It typically includes liability insurance, which frees your landlord from liability from any harm you may experience and covers all your business equipment and furniture located in your office. A lease company or landlord may ask to see a copy of your business insurance policy before renting space to you.

Workers' compensation insurance is separate from the insurance policies that are protecting your business and its assets because it is related to your employees. *Learn more about insurance options in Chapter 12.*

When seeking an insurance company, find a reputable one that is licensed and experienced in business insurance, preferably staffed by agents who deal with businesses. Obtain policy price quotes from at least three to five companies and make sure each one takes the time to tailor a policy suitable for your needs with a range of plans and options. If you are not sure what type of insurance to purchase, an experienced insurance agent can help determine your needs and which policy or policies would be best. Insurance companies want your business, so if you run across an agent who is unaccommodating, take your business needs elsewhere. If the agent is unwilling to answer your questions, you should not choose him or her to insure your business; this insurance agent will not be giving you the best insurance options for your business. The best agent will be truly interested in the best and most appropriate insurance coverage for your business, and he or she will be knowledgeable about the right type of coverage to meet your business needs.

Business equipment

It might be a good idea to purchase a new computer as your first business expense to keep your business computer separate from your home computer. This is important when considering the space available on a new computer and the speed. Even if your home computer is just a few years old, a new one will put you at an advantage when beginning your medical billing business. Your new computer will be most likely be pre-loaded with basic software you need for a business. If this computer is purchased specifically for your medical billing business, it is tax-deductible because it will be a business expense.

Here is some information pertaining to major equipment purchases:

Computer: The most integral component of your business will be the computer. The vast majority of billing will be done electronically, and even if you submit paper forms, you will still need your computer to obtain coding information, generate invoices, research, submit claims, and more. If you have an existing computer, you should evaluate it in terms of its performance capabilities and how old it is. You can upgrade your current computer, but if not, you may need to buy a new one.

If you intend to purchase a new computer, be sure to choose one that is sufficient to manage the billing software package that you will be utilizing. The major computer components include the hard drive, memory card, and processor. The hard drive stores all of your data and will have a storage capacity ranging from 40 GB to 500 GB. A hard drive with more storage capacity is more expensive; however, it is imperative the computer is able to accommodate increased file storage needs as your business expands. It is best to buy a computer with the most storage capacity that you can find.

The memory card determines the speed at which your computer processor runs. The current recommended minimum amount of memory is 516 MB, although larger memory cards with 1 GB, 2 GB, or 2.5 GB are available. The computer processor runs all of your programs. One of the most common processors is the Intel® Pentium Processor, which ensures high-speed processing and the ability to run multiple processes simultaneously, making it ideal for medical billing.

The most simplified way to ensure you have everything you need is to purchase a computer package that includes a computer, printer, various software programs, and miscellaneous items like a scanner or Web camera — all for one price. You may purchase a computer package from huge chain electronics stores or have a local computer store build you a computer with just what you need, and there are usually excellent computer packages for sale online. Basic desktop and laptop computer packages range from $500 to $1,200, depending on your storage capacity and other options

Software: If you choose to take care of your own taxes and accounting, you might want to consider buying a top-rated financial software program, like Quicken™ or Quickbooks™. TurboTax® and TaxWise are also two programs useful for figuring out how much tax you owe. These are just a few of the financial and tax software programs available. If you are too overwhelmed by the choices or feel that your taxes are too complicated, then you can always call an accountant to do the work for you. Another type of software you will need is security and spam protection software. When purchasing spam protection and computer security software, remember that you need to keep your customer's business information absolutely safe, so do not skimp on it. Buy the best software to ensure your customers' medical claims information is safe. Check your medical billing software to see if it includes security features. If it does, see if there is a need for additional security software. You must make sure you have adequate security protection to make sure you are keeping your patients' files secure and complying with HIPAA standards.

Backup: One of the most important and valuable things to do for your business is to make sure you back up your files daily so that if your computer crashes, files can be recovered. Many companies now offer online computer backup services, which are convenient, secure and, in many cases, automatic. If your computer crashes (e.g., if there is an overnight power outage due to a thunderstorm) and all of the claims you worked on that morning were not backed up because you did not have time to do so before the power went out, they are easily retrieved by going online and providing your password. These online backup services can back up all of your files daily for a small monthly fee. You can find them easily by doing an Internet search for "online backup service providers." There are also small flash drives for backup, and they may work at first, but eventually your medical billing files may be too much for a flash drive. You should also purchase an external drive to back up your files daily, like a zip drive. It is probably best to start with a large backup source so that you do not have to switch backup services or methods at some point.

Surge protector: A surge protector will help keep your equipment safe and free from damage if lightning strikes. You should take all the necessary precautions to protect all your equipment and data. Buy the largest capacity surge protector available for the best protection.

Printer: Because the majority of claims will be filed electronically, a printer will be used primarily for client invoices and patient billing. You will also have to print any paper claim forms insurance companies require. Depending on the size of your business, a small capacity inkjet printer will be adequate, or you can purchase a laser printer for high-volume printing. Be sure to choose a printer with affordable ink cartridges. Printers can be purchased from as low as $50 and can increase to $200 or more. If you would like to have a paper-free office, purchase a high-quality printer/scanner, or purchase a separate optical character recognition (OCR) scanner, which converts electronic images into text or legible words you are able to edit.

OCRs are usually quite small and are well-suited for a desktop. Be sure to invest in a high-quality one for accurate, precise scanning.

Copy machine: Many printers now have copier capabilities. For the best deal, you can find a high-quality printer/scanner/copier/fax combination. If you expand into a larger office with employees, you will need a copier on a regular basis for all of your internal business forms, tax forms, personnel information, training materials, advertising, and marketing materials. Copiers can be purchased at office equipment stores as well as at discount and online stores.

Fax machine: A fax machine can save you time and money. If documentation with your signature needs to be sent immediately but cannot be sent electronically, the fax machine becomes a valuable tool. You may also want to have a designated phone line for the fax machine so you will not have to worry about being on the phone or the Internet if someone wants to fax you something. Fax machines can be purchased at office supply stores or discount stores, starting at around $60 for a basic, low-end fax machine. Many Internet service providers or other companies now offer faxing through computers, otherwise known as electronic faxing or e-faxing. This might be a viable option for your business needs because if faxes are sent through a computer, they will not disrupt telephone service.

Scanner: You will definitely need a scanner for your business due to the amount of paperwork that is involved in the medical billing business. If your fax machine or copier does not include a scanner, buy a separate scanner. Be sure to get one that has excellent OCR capabilities because you will have a lot of documents to scan. An OCR will help you scan them accurately so the words are legible.

Phone: Consider having a separate phone line for your fax machine, as you will be sending and receiving faxes and do not want to have to keep the phone line clear for an incoming fax. Most phone companies and many phone systems offer voicemail service, which you should utilize when you are not available. You will be able to access your voicemail from any telephone. If you are planning to hire employees, it is a good idea to have at least two phones lines so that at least two people can be on the phone at the same time. When purchasing a phone for your business, you should consider one that is equipped for more than one line and with speakerphone capability so you can talk while typing. You can also purchase a headset or earpiece for the phone.

DSL service: High-speed Internet service is imperative to any business that is based on electronic activity. A high-speed connection is accessed through a cable modem and allows you to talk on the phone while you are using the Internet. Many cable companies offer high-speed Internet and great packages to choose from, including cable TV, telephone, and dedicated high-speed Internet service. With a dial-up Internet connection, you cannot talk on the phone and be online at once. A digital subscriber line, or DSL, will cost you a little more than a dial-up connection, but the convenience is worth it, and the expense is tax-deductible for your business. The cost depends on the carrier (usually a local or national telephone or cable company) and on the geographic location.

Postage meter: A postage meter will come in handy if you are serving many health care providers and sending large volumes of mail. Another convenient option is to purchase postage online through the U.S. Postal Service℠ (USPS). Consider using a postage meter when you start mailing advertisements, surveys, and bulk mail; it will save you a lot of trips to the post office.

You can lease a postage meter from your local post office or go online to purchase postage. A postage meter enables you to print postage and/or shipping labels from your computer. Below are a list of vendors who provide shipping service and postage meters:

- **U.S. Postal Service: www.usps.com/onlinepostage/welcome. htm** — Print postage and labels online; select "Click 'N Ship" to print labels for Express Mail™ or Priority Mail®; you will need to download one-time software to print labels. Free shipping supplies can be ordered as well.

- **Stamps.com: www.stamps.com/welcome** — To calculate and print official U.S. Postal Service postage directly from your computer, you need an Internet connection, a printer, and their software; no additional hardware is needed, and there is only one monthly fee of about $16.

- **Endicia: www.endicia.com** — Use a free 30-day trial from Endicia to mail envelopes and small packages, compute exact postage, and print customized mailing labels. After the free trial is over, the service costs about $10 a month. You can use this service with both a Mac and a PC.

- **Pitney Bowes™: www.pitneyworks.com** — Use ShipStream postage software to ship packages directly from your computer; refill your postage online any time; track your shipping expenses; or purchase digital postal meters and scales. This requires free downloadable postage software.

Aside from the equipment mentioned in this chapter and all the medical billing-related equipment from Chapter 4, below is a list of office supplies that should be on-hand at all times:

- Stationery

- Brochures about your business

- Fliers about your business

- Business cards

- Envelopes

- Mailing labels

- Pens and pencils

- Folders

- Stapler and staples

- Notebooks

- Income ledgers

- Filing cabinets and filing folders

- Ink cartridges for printer and fax

- CMS 1500 forms

- Postage

- Highlighters

Staying Organized

One of the most important rules in owning a new medical billing business is to stay organized. Simplify your business so when a client calls and needs your assistance, you are able to locate any documents you might need to help your client. Doing the following will help you be consistently organized:

- Record all payments received and distributed; immediately note payments and track them (preferably using business financial software).

- Distribute a meeting agenda prior to each and every business meeting with a client in order to keep track of meeting time, place, and date, and notify staff of the meeting.

- Keep track of the claims that have been sent (this will be done with your medical billing software). Make special note of claims that have been rejected (this can also be done using the medical billing software).

- Keep track of past-due patient accounts (this will be done with your medical billing software).

- Designate a separate file folder for each client; keep contracts and all correspondence filed in here.

- Make a separate file for each individual insurance company for which you file claims (again, keep contracts and all correspondence filed in here).

- Make a file for each employee with complete application, orientation information, and résumé (goes without saying if required by law). Of course, this only applies if you have expanded your business to include employees. *Learn more about hiring employees in Chapter 12.*

- When you take messages, record them in a message receipt booklet so they are not scattered everywhere and so you can call people back in a timely manner.

- Keep desks neat and organized.

- All papers should be filed daily and in the right place.

Always save forms, documents, and files that pertain to the IRS, your medical billing clients, and employees, but shred unwanted and obsolete papers (papers that you are no longer using or documents for former clients) so they are not taking up space. Files that need to be saved can be transferred to a storage area for easy accessibility, or old file contents can be scanned and stored on your computer.

Be sure to file and store items in alphabetic order so it will be easy to find them. If you choose to have a paper-free office, then all documents and files you use or have used will need to be scanned and stored. Look into electronic document storage solutions and off-site electronic storage in order to ensure the safety of documents. You will also need to have an efficient and reliable computer back-up system to safely store all your documents and files.

You can also stay organized with your Web site and e-mail. If you utilize Microsoft® Outlook® Express for e-mail, you can create folders to file incoming e-mails by sender or client name, date, or subject. You can designate files for certain clients, important account information, and other e-mails that come in. This method will help you to eliminate junk mail and spam, and keep your e-mail inbox from overflowing. When someone e-mails you, you will be able to file the e-mail after answering it. Save messages and reference them later if needed.

After receiving financing and getting your business in order, evaluate whether you are following all the national and state employment laws. You do not want to be forced to shut down your business because of a legal oversight.

Legal Considerations

When starting a new medical billing business, you must make sure you abide by the rules and regulations that affect your business in your town, city, or state, such as laws governing the type of business you may open in your home, and rules and regulations regarding licensing your medical billing business. You are advised to contact an attorney to make sure you are following all the laws; IRS and state tax rules and regulations; and all your state and local government agencies' rules, guidelines, and regulations. An attorney can verify that all of your business contracts are legal and other aspects of your business are all sound. An attorney will ensure that you are protected from lawsuits, that you have registered your business name properly, have filed the right taxes, have purchased the correct insurance policies, and have filed and paid for the right licenses and permits. It would also be a good idea to ask your attorney to review the business contracts you will be offering your clients.

Business copyrights

Copyright will protect your work from being copied and used by others, and will give you the authority to pursue legal recourse against those who may infringe on your materials. No one will be allowed to duplicate any of your work for any reason without your permission. The copyright protection laws are incredibly useful when it comes to all the written works that you and your employees will create for your medical billing business in regard to advertising, sales, and marketing. The contents of your Web site, newsletters, brochures, business cards, postcards, and more are protected. Everything you write or create, such as your ideas, comments, and work posted on your Web site, should be copyright protected. According to the U.S. Copyright Office, copyright is a form of protection that insures someone's original work. This includes work from authors, writers, artists, and musicians.

A copyright is automatically secured at the time the work is created; for example, the advertising copy that you wrote for postcards you plan to mail to prospective clients is automatically copyrighted. No registration or publication is required to copyright anything unless you choose to do so. Registration allows the copyright owner to record the registration with the U.S. Customs Service to protect against the importation of infringing copies. Electronic (online) copyright registration is the cheapest method at $35.

IRS requirements

At some point, every business has to deal with the IRS. If you have decided not to use an accountant for your medical billing business, you may want to consider one during tax time. You should meet and select an accountant before tax time (the first quarter of every calendar year prior to April 15 is considered tax time). Your accountant will know what to do, what to deduct, and make sure there are no errors; the IRS does not like mistakes. If you decide to be your own accountant, then come tax time, make sure you are well-aware of what you should be doing; try to find a good accountant who will be available to answer any questions you may have. There are many tax software programs available online, or you can purchase one for your business. These programs tell you step by step what to do and ask for various pieces of information, then determine, based on that, what additional forms are needed. They are better than trying to figure out your taxes by yourself. *See Chapter 4 for more on accounting software choices.*

As with any business, you must register with the IRS and file taxes. If you go on to the IRS Web site (**www.irs.gov**), there is a link for "Starting a Business." Here you will be able to follow the rules and guidelines for beginning your own business. The IRS expects you to select a business structure after deciding if your business is for-profit or not-for-profit; a medical billing business would be for-profit. Once you have decided on the entity, this will help you decide which tax returns you will have to file, and once you have accomplished this, you will then need to file for an EIN. This will help show which entity you are. You can apply for this online.

Numbers are issued free by the IRS; businesses that operate as a partnership or corporation and have employees (even just one) need one. The Internet EIN application is the preferred method for customers to apply for and obtain an EIN. Once the application is completed, the information is validated during the online session, and an EIN is issued immediately. The online application process is available for all entities whose principal business, office or agency, or legal residence (in the case of an individual), is located in the United States or U.S. territories.

The taxes that may be associated with your medical billing business are:

- **Income tax** — Tax based on the amount of income your business earns

- **Excise tax** — A tax on various commodities or service a business may offer

- **Employment tax** — If you have employees, you must file a certain form and pay certain taxes

- **Self-employment tax** — Required from business owners who have net earnings of $600 or more annually

As your medical billing business grows, you may eventually have to pay quarterly income taxes, based on income you earn every quarter (the amount is usually based on income received during the same time last year). This will help you avoid paying a huge amount once a year to the IRS, but it does mean more paperwork — and one more thing you (or your accountant) must do.

Another aspect of the IRS you will have to deal with is the chance of being audited. An audit is a formal check of your business' financial records and can occur at any time.

Auditing

The reason for an audit is to make sure your financial statements are accurate and honest. The IRS is also checking to make sure there are no errors in your financial statements and to make sure you are doing them correctly. If you are being audited, you can contact someone who has been audited or do a lot of research so you can pass your audit. Your accountant can also help you through it. The consequences of a negative audit are that you may have to pay a fine or pay an additional amount to the IRS.

If you do get audited, the IRS will request the following:

- Financial statements

- Bank statements

- Business receipts (for expenses)

Keep everything filed by year, and keep your financial paperwork where you can find it easily. If you are audited, make sure you have prepared your paperwork before the auditor arrives. Be sure to save all receipts and tax forms prepared by your accountant, as the IRS can audit you for the last three years.

Licenses and Zoning Requirements

There are no federal licensing requirements for a medical billing service. Business licenses vary from state to state, so it is recommended you contact your secretary of state's office. Your town or city might have rules and regulations that you have to abide by to run a business.

Check your state's list of special occupational business licenses to see if your state requires a license for a medical billing business. This list should be on the secretary of state's Web site, or linked to it by another state-governing organization. Zoning regulations and signage issues are usually under local law in every state.

At this point, you have finally done it — you now have your medical billing business up and running. After all the start-up steps have been completed, you must now focus on ways to keep your business running efficiently and turning a profit. The next chapter takes a look at operations and covers just about everything you need to know to open your business's doors.

Chapter 9

Operations

This chapter will teach you about day-to-day operations of your medical billing business and where you can turn if you need advice with your new business venture. Once you figure out what needs to be done and what is the most important task to get done each day, such as submitting claims, you will be able to figure out your agenda.

Some MIBs prefer to work locally, while others like to expand their services nationwide. There is nothing wrong with that; however, you are limited geographically as far as potential clients if you choose to only work with local clients. Having a local business is beneficial when you need something and can jump in your car and drive over to your client's office. It is a good idea when you are starting out to begin with local doctors' offices as your first clients. Once you have a stable, working relationship established with them, you will have references for when you are ready to expand your business. But regardless of whether you have a local business or a national one, one of the most important areas to consider when establishing your business' daily routine are the hours your business will be open.

Hours of Operation

When owning and operating a business, you will want to operate with set hours. Clients need to know that someone will be available to answer their questions during the usual business hours (typically 9 a.m. to 5 p.m.). Keep your hours of operation consistent; taking a lunch is fine, but coming in at 12 p.m. when you were supposed to be there at 9 a.m. and leaving at 2 p.m. when you were supposed to leave at 5 p.m. is not feasible. Of course, if you make use of an answering machine (and return your calls) or always have a cell phone with you to take calls, that will help you operate with more flexible business hours should you need to leave work early one day or come in a little late because of an unexpected emergency.

Accounting and Bookkeeping

Accounting and bookkeeping are important parts of your medical billing business. Accounting enables you to keep track of your income and your expenses. If your funds permit, you can always hire an accountant or a bookkeeper to keep track of all the numbers. The best place to help you find an accountant are your local yellow pages. It is crucial to keep track of all of your financial records for your business, especially to help you file your taxes and in case the IRS ever audits you. If you do not know basic accounting, there are classes you can take at a local college or university and software programs you can buy at your local office supply store. *See Chapter 4 for information about accounting software programs.*

Evaluating your finances

Periodically, you will need to evaluate your business finances, as well as review reports, income statements, loss statements, expense statements, petty cash records, and accounting records. If you find any errors, you can correct them before they interrupt your business. You need to make sure everything is running properly and your business is running the way it should be run. If something is out of the ordinary, you will need to make the appropriate changes.

An effective tool to help you with evaluating your business is the income statement, which allows you to record business profits and losses. You can choose to evaluate the statements as often as you would like, but you are responsible for keeping a daily income statement called a ledger. You can evaluate the ledger monthly, bimonthly, or every three months, but monthly is best in order to keep a close eye on your business and income, Below are two statements you can use to keep track of your profits and losses.

Income statement for (Business Name)

Client _____ Date _____ Amount _____ Initial _____
Client _____ Date _____ Amount _____ Initial _____
Client _____ Date _____ Amount _____ Initial _____
Client _____ Date _____ Amount _____ Initial _____
Client _____ Date _____ Amount _____ Initial _____
Client _____ Date _____ Amount _____ Initial _____
Client _____ Date _____ Amount _____ Initial _____
Client _____ Date _____ Amount _____ Initial _____
Client _____ Date _____ Amount _____ Initial _____
Client _____ Date _____ Amount _____ Initial _____
Client _____ Date _____ Amount _____ Initial _____
Client _____ Date _____ Amount _____ Initial _____
Client _____ Date _____ Amount _____ Initial _____
Client _____ Date _____ Amount _____ Initial _____
Client _____ Date _____ Amount _____ Initial _____
Client _____ Date _____ Amount _____ Initial _____
Client _____ Date _____ Amount _____ Initial _____
Client _____ Date _____ Amount _____ Initial _____
TOTAL AMOUNT RECEIVED _____

This is your profit statement, or money generated from clients. Write down who has paid you, the amount received, and the date received. A daily profit statement will keep track of your income daily, and no questions will arise if you keep such close track of income.

Below is an expense statement, which is your loss statement. This statement is designated for bills that you pay, supplies that you buy, accounting fees, taxes, and anything you pay out of your business. It is highly advisable to record it daily so there are no questions asked a week from now about what bill was paid, when, how much, and by whom. All bills that are paid should be initialed, and all income that has been accepted should be initialed. Include bank deposits and withdrawals in this equation.

Whatever expenses you pay for should also be recorded and the receipts saved for your accountant. If you pay to license your business name, that is a business expense and should be recorded. This will help you keep track of your business expenses.

Expense statement for (Business Name)

Expense _____	Date _____	Amount _____	Initial _____
Expense _____	Date _____	Amount _____	Initial _____
Expense _____	Date _____	Amount _____	Initial _____
Expense _____	Date _____	Amount _____	Initial _____
Expense _____	Date _____	Amount _____	Initial _____
Expense _____	Date _____	Amount _____	Initial _____
Expense _____	Date _____	Amount _____	Initial _____
Expense _____	Date _____	Amount _____	Initial _____
Expense _____	Date _____	Amount _____	Initial _____
Expense _____	Date _____	Amount _____	Initial _____
Expense _____	Date _____	Amount _____	Initial _____
Expense _____	Date _____	Amount _____	Initial _____
Expense _____	Date _____	Amount _____	Initial _____
Expense _____	Date _____	Amount _____	Initial _____
Expense _____	Date _____	Amount _____	Initial _____
Expense _____	Date _____	Amount _____	Initial _____
Expense _____	Date _____	Amount _____	Initial _____
Expense _____	Date _____	Amount _____	Initial _____
Expense _____	Date _____	Amount _____	Initial _____

TOTAL AMOUNT EXPENSES PAID OUT _____

You can purchase a business expense book at an office store, which will help you keep track of all the business expenses you have paid, or you can use the sample provided here. Here is a list of sample business expenses:

- Utility bills for your office or home (if your office is in your home)

- The cost of forms that you must buy or submit

- Printing and mailing costs for advertising and marketing materials; bills and letters sent to clients; and paychecks that might need to be mailed

- Auto expenses, such as gas and repairs on the vehicle that you use to run business errands

- Lunch meetings with potential or current clients

- Payroll (should you expand and hire employees)

- Office supplies

The expense book or software will have a place to list the following:

- What was the expense?

- What was the date it was paid?

- What was the amount of the expense?

- Who authorized it?

Make sure when you are working with both statement sheets you add your profit and subtract your expenses; the balance will be your profit or loss. In the beginning, expect there will be more expenses and loss than profit.

Business bank account

Every business needs a banking account. Your business's bank account is how you will cash checks, record deposits, and pay your bills. There are several types of bank accounts to choose from to manage your money. When you start to receive payments for your services, you will need a plan for the money received. One option is to find a bank and talk with a banking consultant who will give you information about all the business accounts. Many banks offer various account options, and you will want to choose the best account that suits your business. Banks also compete for customers, so use that to your advantage by monitoring advertisements and choosing the bank that offers the best rates and terms for your business banking needs.

A checking account will enable you to pay bills for your business and make deposits to cover your debts. Along with this account, you will receive checks and a debit card (if requested). This card can only be used when you have funds available in your account. Overdraft protection is also a good thing to have because if you make a purchase without enough funds in your account, rather than being unable to purchase that item, the bank essentially will fund you the money, which you will have to pay back in addition to a fee.

A business savings account can be used to save money for new software, emergency funds, or whatever you may need it for. When your income is low, you will have something to go back on if you have savings. Both of these accounts should benefit your business. With these accounts, you will be able to accept credit card transactions, checks, money orders, cashier's checks, and PayPal funds from business clients.

Do not overlook online banks, which are banks with an online presence only. They may be just what you need if you prefer to conduct your business online and electronically. If you feel secure in handling your banking and bill payments online, then an online bank might be the right choice. Many of them offer better interest rates than community banks and credit unions, and are easily accessible, always open, and very efficient.

These questions will help you choose the right bank for your business:

1. Is the bank close to you?

2. How many branches does it have (in this area or farther away)?

3. Does it offer business checking and business savings accounts?

4. Does it carry Federal Deposit Insurance Corporation (FDIC) insurance? (FDIC is a government agency that insures every bank deposit up to $250,000 at its member banks, so be sure whatever bank you join is a member)

5. What are its fees for business account options and services?

6. How is its customer service?

7. What hours is the bank open?

8. What are the drive-thru teller hours (if the bank has a drive-thru teller option)?

9. How long does it take deposits to clear?

10. Does it offer business accounts online so you can have instant access to your accounts?

Petty cash

The petty cash fund is a source of money you should have on-hand for incidentals such as deliveries, office supplies, postage, and other necessities. One person, usually the business owner, should be in charge of it. You should keep a log of how much is given to whom, the date, and the purpose. This procedure helps if some of the cash comes up missing or if there has been a mistake made. The person in charge of the petty cash should also be in charge of the receipt book, which is a ledger that has duplicate pages to help keep track of petty cash. A signature should be required for all petty cash disbursements so that if there is a question about anything, there is a signature for every petty cash transaction, which will help determine what kind of transaction took place.

Profit Planning

Profit planning is a way to focus on growth, development, operations, and management of your business. Through profit planning, you will be able to see how your income has increased, decreased, or stayed the same. Profit planning entails developing a projection for your business' gross profit; developing a budget for your operating expenses; and estimating your net profit so you can determine if the profits you make are enough to keep your business in operation. Profit planning is based on estimates and projections, so you should be aware your plan may need to be altered to accommodate unexpected changes. Factors you would want to assess are:

- Are you getting more clients?

- Is the number of clients the same?

- Have you been losing clients?

- Are you losing income?

- Are you able to pay the bills and manage your business better?

Profit planning will help you to see the changes of your business and identify what needs to change to help your profits climb. In order to continue profit planning, you must know what goal you must reach (such as how many claims you should process each month) to help your medical billing business thrive and see a good profit-planning report. Evaluating your profit plan will also help you determine if there are any upcoming issues that will need to be identified and addressed, such as decreasing profit due to loss of a client or purchasing expensive software or a new computer system, which will affect profit.

Some of the advantages to profit planning include:

- It can identify excessive costs

- Problems can be identified early

- It is a good business performance evaluator

- It can help a business owner become aware of his or her various responsibilities (which may have been overlooked)

- You can plan ahead for business growth

- It can inspire investor and lender confidence

You must think about the future often and how you will secure your medical billing business success. You want to achieve and accomplish goals that will help your business succeed. There are companies offering profit planning education, and they can help you take full advantage of excelling in your business. Some Web sites that can help you learn more about profit planning are listed below.

Village Mall's Web site (**www.villagemall.com.au/content/smallbus/profit_planning.htm**) has a feature called "Developing a Profit Plan for Your Business" that will help you develop a business profit plan. This page tells site visitors the usefulness of a profit plan, its limitations, and advantages versus disadvantages. You can learn how to develop a forecast for sales and profit, develop a budget for operation expenses, and estimate your net profit.

The Profit Planning Group helps firms maximize profits, and offers educational programs that provide answers to your questions, like "How much profit should we make?" and "How fast can my business grow?" This company's Web site (**www.profitplanninggroup.com/index.shtml**) allows visitors to print copies of recent profit planning seminars and even offers businesses the option of having one of the group's consultants conduct a study or educational program for their business.

SCORE is an organization that assists small businesses across the country. It offers a 60-second guide to profit planning online (**www.score.org/60_ seconds_to_profit.html**) that is quick and easy to read. Other helpful material includes information about starting and growing your business, managing your business, and ways to finance your new venture.

Leading the Company

One of the most important things you will have to do on a daily basis is lead your company to success. As a leader of the company, you will be in charge of the way your company will run and grow. Whatever decisions you make will affect your business for good or bad, meaning your choices will affect your business long-term and short-term. Each decision should be thought through very carefully.

All clients (and employees once you expand to hire them) will look to you for guidance. You should show respect in order to receive it, always taking your client's or employee's feeling and reactions into consideration. You will want your business to thrive and without proper intelligence, education, and respect, it will not.

Now that you know what your daily operations will entail to keep your business running smoothly internally, you should focus on ways to grow your business by attracting more clients. Advertising and marketing, the subjects of the next chapter, will help you strategize ways to help your business grow.

Chapter 10

Advertising and Marketing

One of the most challenging aspects about your business is finding clients; advertising and marketing will be the keys to your success. Without clients, you do not have a medical billing business, so you will need to be a salesperson for your company.

Marketing is a way of making your business known. Target clients by letting them know about your business, what services it offers, and that you are reliable. You will never quit advertising; it will be an ongoing job from day one. Your business will pick up more as you learn to advertise it and market it. At the beginning, 90 percent of your work will be to sell your business, and the best way to do this is to create a marketing plan.

Developing a Marketing Plan

Your marketing plan does not have to be extensive. Make sure you create a marketing plan that you will use; do not just put together one for the sake of saying that you have one, only to never look at again. Take the time to think through potential avenues and methods of marketing your medical insurance billing business, how it can be done, and how it will be done. Ask someone (your spouse, friend, or mentor) to review your marketing plan and add their ideas, along with correcting any grammar and punctuation errors. These are ten parts to developing a marketing plan for your medical billing business:

- **Market research** — List your potential customers, services you will offer, and market dynamics.

- **Target market** — Describe your business's niche market or the market you are hoping will be interested in your product or service.

- **Product** — Describe your product or service, what your market needs, what it uses, and what it needs above and beyond current products and services available.

- **Competition** — Describe competition and your unique selling proposition. What makes your business stand out from competitors?

- **Mission statement** — This should include whom you are selling to, what you are selling, and your unique selling proposition.

- **Marketing strategies** — Write down the marketing strategies you want to use (such as advertising, trade shows, Web site, direct marketing, and so on).

- **Pricing, positioning, and branding** — The information you have written already should be enough to help you develop strategies to determine product and service pricing, its position in the market, and how to accomplish brand awareness.

- **Budget** — What marketing strategies can you afford? What type of marketing can you do internally to save money? What needs to be outsourced?

- **Marketing goals** — Establish marketing goals, like gaining 30 new clients or increasing your income by 40 percent. Goals can include profits, sales, or customer satisfaction.

- **Monitor your results** — Survey customers; track leads, sales, Web site visitors, and so on to see what marketing strategies are working and what is not working.

After you develop your marketing strategy, you will want to develop a business logo. This logo can and should be used on all your marketing materials so potential clients can familiarize themselves with your company and the services you offer.

Your Business Logo

A logo is a symbol or name of a company or an organization. You will use your business logo on advertising material, letterheads and envelopes, your Web site, and signs. You will want your company's logo to be recognizable, memorable, and easy to spot. Simplicity is the key to logo design; too many colors and shapes will make the design too complicated or jumbled.

If you would rather not handle designing your company's logo and marketing and advertising materials, it might be worth the cost to hire a designer or advertising agency to handle all of this for you so everything will be professionally designed and handled from the start; you will not have to do it if it is something you are not experienced in. You will be paying an agency for its expertise to design a logo and brochure, flier, postcard, business card, Web site, and more according to your criteria.

A smaller advertising firm might charge you less because it will have lower overhead expenses, or you might not paying the money for a large, reputable advertising agency's talent and expertise. Also, you might be fortunate enough to find a one-person design firm or advertising agency in your area that will most likely have lower costs than a larger firm or agency (check your phone book under "advertising agencies" or "public relations firms"). This one-person agency may be very talented at designing logos and marketing material, so do not disregard them. If you know someone who has offered to provide the design for your written advertising and marketing materials, be cautious. Ask for references and ask to see similar material the designer has done for another company. Just because someone knows how to use their computer's design program does not mean they will produce something you want to mail to prospective clients.

After you have developed a marketing plan and created a logo, you will want to use these items to find clients to help your medical billing business grow.

Finding Clients

One way you can look for new clients is to advertise to any and all health care providers. Start with the local yellow pages or your hospital's local physicians' directory. You might also consult Medicare's *Physician and Other Healthcare Professional Directory* (online at **www.medicare.gov**). Physicians can be selected by location, so you can advertise to local ones first and then expand. An efficient way to begin your advertising campaign is to purchase labeling software and stickers and create a mailing list of all the names and addresses you have pulled from the local yellow pages, hospital physicians' directory, and Medicare's *Physician and Other Healthcare Professional Directory.* Each time you decide to launch a direct mail marketing campaign or send out any marketing materials, you can make labels from your mailing list.

Here is a list of common marketing and advertising strategies you can use for your medical billing campaign. All of these strategies will be explained in more detail later in the chapter.

- **Direct mail marketing campaign:** This involves sending out letters, advertisements, and brochures about your business to potential clients.

- **Cold calls/cold visits:** It is a good idea to visit at least two doctors' offices a week and leave your business card there. If the doctor needs a medical biller six months from now or 18 months from now, he or she will have your card. Do not hesitate to revisit offices every year or so to leave your card.

- **Phone surveys:** This is a convenient way to call and speak to the doctor and ask about his or her medical billing. The doctor will probably not have time to speak with you, but if he or she does, consider yourself a lucky person; use your time wisely. Ask the doctor if he or she has a medical biller for his or her practice, and how satisfied he or she is with his or her services. Ask him or her if you can mail a brochure in case the current medical biller does not work out. Let him or her also know what type of services you offer and your fees.

- **E-mails:** This is another convenient way to sell your business, but remember that with e-mail, it is very easy to say no. Your e-mail should explain (briefly) who you are and what services your company provides that will lighten their workload. Include your rates, how reliable you are, and how quickly you can get claims paid.

- **Word-of-mouth from current clients:** This is one of the best ways to get clients because it is a simple marketing and advertising strategy. To use word-of-mouth advertising, provide exceptional services to your existing clients, and they in turn will tell their colleagues and friends about the outstanding service you provided for them. Potential clients will come to you because another professional is pleased with your company and told them about it.

- **A booth at medical conferences:** This is one way to meet hundreds of doctors. Ask them about their satisfaction with their current MIB. Offer your business card and flier, and ask for their business cards to follow up in a week or so. This would be a great opportunity to pass out fliers with special rates or services for new customers. You might offer to speak at different medical conferences or programs where topics relate to medical billing, medical records, or insurance. This way, you can promote your knowledge and your business name to thousands of medical providers across the country.

Most likely other medical billing companies will offer the same services you do, so be sure you tell prospective clients what makes your company stand out above the competition. Tell them why your company can provide better claims submission services (e.g., because you are certified in three areas and because you have worked in the industry for 20 years, or whatever it is that makes your company the best).

You will need to find the right place to start and research the market and economy where you are located. Focus on high-population, high-income communities where the residents have money for non-essential doctor visits, particularly to plastic surgeons. You can even go outside of the box and think worldwide; you do not have to stay local. Your computer, e-mail, and fax machine can go all over the world, so that means you can, too.

One of the first ways you should try finding new clients is through a direct mail marketing campaign. Direct mail is the easiest form of marketing that can help you find clients.

Direct Mail Campaigns

You can mail surveys to your target clients and tell the recipients to mail them back in the self-addressed stamped envelope (SASE) you include in the mailing. If you are mailing surveys, they will be along the lines of the sample provided below, asking about their current level of medical billing services, and explaining what your company offers. Other direct mail can be any marketing material, including brochures, postcards, fliers, or a newsletter. Do not misspell anything; use professional language and proper grammar; and make your message short and concise. Once you have a client's interest, you will need to prove why your business is good and what makes it stand out from the others. When you have the interest of the doctor, this is the time to work exceptionally hard to prove you are capable of taking on his/her business.

On the following page is an example of a survey that you might want to send out after starting your company. It will help you know the level of satisfaction in the local marketplace with local billing companies. It is also a nice way to let physicians know that there is a new medical billing business in the area — one that might be better than their current service provider.

SAMPLE BUSINESS SURVEY

Your Medical Billing Company's Name
Address
City, state, ZIP code
Phone number
Fax number

Date
Client's name
Address
City, state, ZIP code

Dear Dr. Doe,
(This section will explain who you are, what services your company provides, and how you can benefit his/her physician practice.)
Below are some questions I would like you to answer and return in the enclosed SASE. If you have indicated that you would like to see improvements in your medical billing practices, I will contact you with a better offer than what you are currently receiving from your present MIB.

How do you file your claims?
☐ A full-time staffer does this for me
☐ A part-time staffer does this for me
☐ I do it myself
☐ It is outsourced

What is your estimated wait time to have a claim paid?
☐ 2 to 4 days
☐ 5 to 7 days
☐ One week
☐ 10 days
☐ 14 days
☐ 30 to 60 days

What is your cost to file per claim?
☐ Less than $1 per claim
☐ Between $1 and $2 per claim
☐ Higher than $2 per claim

What is the average number of claims billed per month?
☐ Fewer than 50
☐ 50 to 100
☐ 101 to 500
☐ More than 500

Would you be interested in having another person or company do your medical billing?
☐ Yes
☐ No

If not, what might change your mind?
☐ Lower rates
☐ Quicker reimbursements
☐ Better service and treatment
☐ Faster claims filing
☐ More/better collections

What services would you like to see a medical insurance biller (MIB) offer?
☐ Claims billing/reimbursement
☐ Practice management
☐ Other (please specify) _____

How do you follow up with rejected claims?
_____
_____

Would you like to take advantage of our special offer (explain the offer here)?
☐ Yes
☐ No

What do you dislike about your current MIB?
☐ Inefficient
☐ Slow
☐ Not knowledgeable about codes and/or claims filing
☐ Too expensive
☐ Not bringing in money owed from old claims

☐ Other _____

☐ I am happy with my current MIB

Would you like more information about our business and all the services we have to offer?

☐ Yes

☐ No

Again, thank you for your time; I know how valuable it is.

Sincerely,

(Your signed name)

Your printed name

Business name

Telephone number

E-mail address

Web address

Be sure all material you mail to prospective clients is held to the highest of standards. Double-check the spelling of the recipient's name and address. Show potential clients you pay particular attention to details so they can see you are detail-oriented and can be trusted to handle the details of their medical claims billing.

Utilizing e-mail

Another direct mail campaign, which is less expensive, is to create an e-mail list of all the local health care providers that you are targeting. The local medical society, hospital, or health care system might provide such a mailing list to you upon request. If not, you can hire a marketing company to put it together, or you can do it yourself.

Do not expect all surveys to be returned, though. Surveys have a low return rate and considering that these are being sent to people who may never have heard of you or your business, you should not expect a high return rate. The information you receive, however, will be invaluable to you as a business owner and may provide you with some prospective clients if you follow up with these prospects diligently and honestly.

Mailing postcards

Postcards are easy and cheap to make and send (postage is cheaper than standard mail). Use a card stock that is heavier than regular copy paper, and make it colorful so it stands out and demands to be read. Put a message on the front as well as the back. Consider using attention-getting messages on your business postcards, like "It's About Your Bills!" and "Good News, Doctor, We Know Exactly What You Should Charge For Your Services! Wouldn't You Like to Know?" You want to capture their attention the instant they turn the card over (probably while preparing to throw it away). Make an offer along with your company name and phone number. You might print something like "Call now for reduced rates."

Brochures

You can plan a mass mailing of brochures to all area physicians. Brochures can either be tri-fold (six pages, front and back) or just one standard letter-size sheet of paper folded in half (four pages, front and back). The brochure should list the following:

- Services you offer
- Hours of operation
- Location
- Why and when you opened your business
- Your experience in medical billing
- Rates
- Specials

- New customer bonus (if applicable)

You can make your own brochures by using a software program that may already be on your computer; if not, you can buy this software at an office supply store. A more professional option that will give potential clients a good first impression would be to hire a graphic designer. You can provide all the information to this person, even write your own brochure information, but depend on the graphic designer to lay it out in an aesthetically pleasing way that will leave readers with a good first impression of your business.

Business Cards

A business card is also very important to your business. It provides clients and potential clients with your business's name, your name, and relevant contact information. You can have business cards printed professionally by a local printer or an online printer.

Your business card should include your business name and logo, your name (designated as owner), certifications, address, phone number, and Web site address. *More about building a Web site will be discussed later in this chapter.* You will also want to include your e-mail address, or if you have a separate e-mail address for your company, include that one instead of your personal e-mail. If you or your business has a page on the social networking sites **www.Facebook.com** or **www.LinkedIn.com**, then include these Web addresses as well. Be sure that your Facebook or LinkedIn site serves a business function, not a personal one.

One of the best Web sites to start with when it comes to getting business cards is **www.vistaprint.com**; you can get 250 free business cards, selecting from more than 42 designs, and only pay for shipping; but there are others to choose from if you do not like the free ones. You can even download your own image or logo for your business cards as well, and the cards will be imprinted with it. Of course, you will pay more if you choose to use your own image or logo, but it is worth it. Another online printing resource is **www.hotcards.com**, where 1,000 two-sided, full-color business cards cost $60. Normal turnaround is two days, but you can get your cards in just one day by paying extra.

The main idea for a business card is to make sure it is bold and stands out, something like below. Keep your business cards updated and take them with you everywhere you go.

Mountainside Billing
(Insert billing specialties)

5555 Mountainside Drive
Columbus, Ohio 43232
Office: 555-555-5555
Fax: 555-555-5555
www.mountainsidebilling.com

If your marketing message will remain the same, along with your company name, address, and phone number, then consider having large quantities printed of each of your written marketing tools, as it is less expensive to buy in bulk. You will eventually use them all (hopefully sooner rather than later) once your marketing campaign is in full swing, which it should be at the beginning of your business.

Cold Visits

This is where you visit a prospective client whom you have never spoken with or met. Your main objective is to speak with the person in charge, namely the doctor or sometimes the office manager. You will probably not be able to speak with the doctor, as he or she will be busy with patients, but offer your card to whomever is kind enough to give you a few minutes to explain your business. Explain your services and how they can help cut the practice's workload. Outline your costs. You should have a brochure with this information; if so, this can help keep your speech short. They can read the brochure later and learn more, but be sure to direct them to your company's Web site. Get the person's business card, and make a note to follow up with him or her in a week or so after you have visited.

When you make the follow-up call or visit, ask if whomever you spoke to has had time to read the brochure and if there are any questions you can answer about your services. If the brochure does not provide information about any special offers, then you can see if he or she is still interested after you explain your company's special offers. You may want to call in another week or two and keep the office on your follow-up list, which is a list of prospective clients that you will plan to call to keep your medical billing company's name and services in their thoughts. You will also send marketing materials to those on your follow-up list. Make sure to contact prospects regularly, whether it is just a making a call or sending a brochure every few months, twice a year, or once a year. Let them know that your business is still there to help them.

Referrals

A referral is when someone refers other people to you for your services; this is also known as word-of-mouth advertising. Referrals normally happen because someone has recommended your services, and when this happens, you should be proud of yourself for having an honest, trustworthy, and reliable business; after all, someone did recommend you. Medical providers all talk to each other, so make sure you do a great job for your current clients, and they will recommend you as often as they can. You can also offer a reward to clients for referring you to other medical providers. Most companies offer some type of referral program, and your company may also benefit from doing so. The reward is issued either right away or after the new prospect has been a customer for 60 days, 90 days, or even six months. You are free to set your own terms if you plan to reward clients for referring others to your company. Advertise and share the rules regarding this bonus reward with your clients as well as in your brochure, newsletters, and all marketing material. Have the rules in writing so if anyone questions them, you will have something to reference.

Following Up

Every potential client needs a follow-up call, visit, or survey. If you send a direct mailing to potential clients and never follow up, you might as well give up on marketing your business. Potential clients are very busy and need you to remind them that you are able to provide some cost-saving benefits and services to their business. You should follow up after you have passed out your brochures and business cards; after you have done your cold calls, direct mailing, and networking; and after you have received referrals.

Because you are keeping track of what material was mailed along with each prospective client's name, clinic name, phone number, and address, you will be able to call them and let them know you sent them a brochure about your business and that you are calling them to follow up. Ask if any of your services were of interest and if they have any questions. If you decide not to call them, you can make a monthly mailing list and keep prospective clients on the list as long as you would like. Eventually you will and should make an effort to meet with them. The idea is if you keep sending advertisements, they will more than likely respond in a couple of different ways: either by calling you and requesting that you stop sending them anything, or calling because they are in a bind and need someone to help with the medical billing.

As Merlin Coslick, founder of the Electronic Medical Billing Network, states in his book: "Persistence alone will produce clients ...if you market to them, they will come."

Networking

If you find that you are having difficulty marketing your business and attracting clients, you may be able to turn to other MIBs and ask how they gained clients when they first started in the industry. Networking is one of the best things that ever happened to the medical billing industry and new business owners. It is easier than ever to talk to someone who has gone through what you are going through. When questions arise — and many of them will — it is wonderful to be able to pick up a phone and ask "How do you do this?" or "Why do I have to do this?" Having connections with other medical billing businesses is very helpful. If you are close to another medical billing business owner, you have wonderful support and resources close by — and you can never have enough support or resources when it comes to your business.

There are all types of medical billing support, resources, and networking available to you online. If a national medical billing industry organization like AHIMA or AAPC does not have a local chapter in your area, contact the organization for help in creating one. It will be a good way for you to find the networking and local support that will help your business grow, and it will be an excellent way to become involved in the industry on a local level. You can also join medical billing organizations once you become certified in the industry. These industry organizations offer help and support for claims or any questions you may have.

Attending a professional organization's annual meeting or conference is a great way to meet people you can exchange advice with; you can also attend educational sessions that will provide you with some good business ideas, from staffing to billing to new legislation. Make time to do this at least once a year, or if you belong to a few professional organizations, maybe alternate the years you attend their conference — attend the AAPC meeting this year, and the AHIMA meeting next year. Most of the professional organizations also have state or regional chapters that meet monthly or bimonthly, closer to home, and with people whom you may know. All of these meetings are a chance to network, learn what is going on in the industry, and learn new things that may help you provide a better service to your clients. They should be taken advantage of as frequently as possible.

Building a Web Site

Creating a Web site for your business may be a challenge, but the results can be great. If you go to an online search engine and type "medical billing," hundreds of medical billing companies will come up. Your company's Web site can be the main source for information and testimonials about your business.

Look at the Web sites of the medical billing companies featured in this book's case studies to give you some ideas for how you want your company's Web site to look. Or you can perform an Internet search to look at the Web sites of other MIBs.

One example is **www.chicagolandmedicalbilling.com,** the Web site for Chicagoland Medical Billing Specialists, Inc. This Web site lists all the services they provide clients and how they enhance the services. The "About Us" page has photos of each of the owners, along with a quote from each about their business's strengths. The Web site design is simple: four pages, four colors, not a huge number of pictures or amount of color to distract visitors, allowing the focus to remain on the important information. The address, name, and phone number are easy to find on the home page.

This will give you an idea of what information to include and how you can build your site. If you are not technology-savvy, this may be one of your biggest challenges. A Web site is one of the most informational and best advertisements for your business because it will show the world what you do, the services you offer, who you are, and your rates. You can ask people to e-mail your business for a price quote and then follow up with those that requested a price quote but have not taken advantage of your services yet.

You can contact a professional Web site designer or graphic designer to build your site, which can be expensive, or you can buy software and do it yourself. If you decide to contract out this project, you will also either have to ensure this person will be available to update the Web site whenever you have changes, or you will have to learn how to do it yourself. Advertising and public relations agencies will be glad to design a Web site for your business, but you will pay a lot of money for it.

A freelance Web designer, however, might be a more affordable option, but first check his or her references and look at other clients' completed Web sites. Be sure this designer has created sites for similar businesses. If you know how you want your site to look, present your idea to him or her. A designer should be open to your idea and work with it. You should type the information just as you want it to appear on your Web site and give it to the designer. Most designers are not strong writers, so they will focus on the design of the site, while you will be responsible for the written content. Some Web site designers might be happy to write the content for you, and some may know a freelance writer who will write the content for your site.

If you decide to design your site yourself, one option is to buy an inexpensive Web site building software program that is self-explanatory, like Web Studio 5.0 (**www.webstudio.com**), or XSitePro, (**www.xsitepro.com**). Web Studio 5.0 offers full Web design functionality with free online content; is easy to use; and lets anyone create professional-looking Web pages quickly. It comes with program CD-ROMs and a video tutorial CD with 24 professionally designed templates for $180. XSitePro has a spell checker, thesaurus, multi-page creation wizard, backup and restore feature, clip art library, dedicated user forum, and more for $197. The software is delivered as an electronic download five minutes after you place your order.

Another option is to use one of the many Web site templates and software programs located online that are easy to find with the help of a search engine, such as **www.eBizwebpages.com** or **www.bluevoda.com**. eBizwebpages.com has no set-up fee; lets you be in control of your Web site; and provides unlimited pages and unlimited updates, many custom designs, professional graphics, and a ten-day free trial. The price depends on the amount of disk space your Web site takes or needs, from 350 MB at $20 per month to up to 1,000 MB for $100 per month. BlueVoda is free and allows you to build your own Web site in 30 minutes with free logos, templates, and page backgrounds from the site's image library. No HTML knowledge is required, and pre-designed Web site templates are included to help you create an unlimited number of Web pages.

These software options are relatively easy to use, but if you want an original and professional-looking site, you are better off hiring someone to do it. A medical professional who may be considering your services might be turned off by a Web site that is not professionally done. Web sites serve a basic need of having a site with basic business information, but most do not conjure a sense of professionalism that your business needs in order to attract clients. You need a site with more than one page that will answer all questions that a potential client might have.

Once the site is built, it will become a key advertisement and source of information about your business. Pay the extra money in the beginning to have your site professionally designed so it will stand out and not make people question your level of professionalism.

Here is a list of items to include on your Web site:

- The services your company offers

- Your mission statement

- Hours of operation

- Your business location

- How potential clients can contact you

- How you started your business

- Why a potential client should choose you

- Your pricing range or specific prices (itemized, if possible)

The most challenging aspect of your Web site will be finding the time to keep it updated. If you are not able to keep it updated, then potential clients looking at it will not have the most up-to-date information about you and your business, which can be frustrating. Potential clients will not be interested in your company if the prices on the Web site are outdated, and they will turn elsewhere for an MIB. You should make sure you keep your Web site updated as often as possible by scheduling yourself to do the weekly updates or being sure the person you are paying to update it is actually doing it when it should be done.

There is a vast amount of potential that a Web site can provide your business, and if you keep it updated, it will work for you.

When building your Web site, you need an online provider to host your files. If you hire someone to design your Web site, he or she will recommend an online host, or you can suggest one yourself. Below are a few national companies that host Web site files, how much they charge, and their set-up fees (these are subject to change):

- **StartLogic: www.startlogic.com/startlogic** — Monthly hosting starts at about $6 per month; setup is free

- **Host Monster: www.hostmonster.com** — Monthly hosting is about $6; setup is free

- **Ix Web hosting: www.ixwebhosting.com** — Monthly hosting for a business is about $8; setup is free

- **Yahoo! Web Hosting: http://smallbusiness.yahoo.com** — Monthly hosting is about $7.50 per month for the first three months (and about $10 per month after the first three months); setup is free

During your process of building a Web site, you will choose a Web site name; normally it will be your medical billing company's name. When someone types in "Medical billing businesses" into a search engine, there are ways to make sure your company's name pops up near the top of every search list, where it will be seen more often. Search engine optimization (SEO) is the practice of overseeing the design or redesign of a Web site so it will attract visitors by winning top ranking on search engines for selected keywords or phrases (like "medical billing companies"). One way to increase your SEO is to hire an SEO company to improve the volume of traffic to your medical billing business Web site by reviewing your site content, providing technical advice on Web site development or redesign, advising you on content development and keyword research, and providing expertise in specific markets. Their price ranges vary widely, and the companies are easily found online. You will have to determine the value of this service to your business, and decide if it is something you want to pursue.

After you have found clients with a successful marketing campaign, you must think of ways to keep them happy. If your customers are not happy, they will not continue to have you handle their medical billing. The next chapter will cover ways to keep your clients loyal to your services and provides simple ideas to help you connect with clients.

Chapter 11

Working with Clients

C lients are the reason for your business, so you will be working with them daily and serving them. You will need to learn how to deal with a grumpy client as well as a needy client. This chapter will teach you how to find your clients, interview them, charge them, assess their needs, and train your employees to serve them.

Meeting Prospective Clients

When a potential client has agreed to meet with you, he or she is interested in your business and what it can do for his or her medical practice. Set up an appointment with your potential client and prepare for this interview. You want to make a great impression and do a wonderful job, proving to your potential client that you have what it takes to represent their practice in filing medical claims. You will have to work hard to prove you are reliable and trustworthy because not all doctors like the idea of giving an account to someone they do not know.

When you go to your interview with a potential client, you should:

- Dress appropriately.

- Be clean and well-groomed.

- Be well-prepared.

- Have a list of questions for your potential client, such as what type of services he or she is receiving now from their current medical biller, what other services he or she would like or need, what he or she expects from a medical billing company, what his or her experience has been with MIBs in the past, and why he or she is looking for another MIB now.

- Make sure the interview is brief yet to the point, and that you have covered everything.

- Provide a brochure and business card, and any other informational material you have about your business.

- Prove to the doctor (or whomever you are interviewing with) that you are able to handle his or her account.

- Ask for a meeting with his or her current MIB to see if there is something you can do to help improve cash flow.

- Ask the doctor to review his or her day sheet and see if you can improve it in any way.

- Ask the doctor if there anything that he or she would like done differently regarding medical billing and claim submissions.

- Ask if you can show that you can do it differently.

- If the client is not happy with his or her current medical biller, assure him or her you will do whatever it takes to win his or her business.

- After the interview, tell him or her that you appreciate his or her time.

- Send a thank-you note showing your appreciation for his or her time.

After a client hires you, make sure you fill out the following form. This form will help you stay organized and allow you to easily access insurance information for each of your clients.

Sample physician sheet

Client's name _____

Practice name _____

Address _____

City _____ State, ZIP _____

Phone (__) _____ Fax (__) _____

E-mail _____

HMOs and group insurance numbers:

_____

_____

_____

_____

_____

_____

_____

_____

_____

_____

_____

_____

_____

_____

Keep this sheet up-to-date because it will help you keep track of all of the physicians' information, and you will be able to add to it as you go. This will help you when submitting claims or when you need to contact the client.

Charging Your Clients Their Claim Fee

After you have started working for your clients, you will have to decide how much to charge them for your services. You can charge your clients by the claim, per hour, or by a certain percentage. When charging a percentage, you will take a percentage of the total amount the doctor has collected from claims that you have filed. If you charge per claim, you may want to do some research to find out how much other MIBs are charging in your area; you do not want your prices to be too low or too high. When you charge per claim, you charge for all claims billed, not collected.

Charging by the hour is not the best method. More than likely, doctors will not want to pay you hourly, as they probably pay all their employees an hourly fee. To process paper claims, it is normally around $20 per claim, and to process electronic claims, it costs around $2 a claim.

You can decide the type of payment after researching what is most common in the industry and what your peers use (perhaps by talking to them through an online forum or by reading about it). You want to make sure what you and your client have agreed on is beneficial to both of you before signing a contract. If you would like to, you can give your client a trial period; if they like you after the trial period is up, they can sign on with your business, and if not, you go your separate ways. If the client does not want to sign, find out why and what you can do to change their decision or what you should do differently. Make sure you will be able to professionally answer all questions your potential clients may have.

When a potential client has agreed to sign a contract to become your client, make sure the contract involves the following:

- What services you will provide for your client

- What types of reports you will send to your client and how often

- Your rates and fees

- When and how often you will bill them

- When payment is due

- Who can terminate the contract and why

Be sure to have a lawyer to look over the contract to make sure everything is legal, accurate, and professional; you can also have a lawyer draw up a standard contract for your business that you can use for each of your clients, unless the terms are different for each client. The professional medical billing organization that you belong to may also have contract templates available for members to access online. If so, that would be a cheaper option than hiring an attorney to draw up a contract, and the contract would have the same legal standing as one written by a lawyer.

What happens if one of your clients refuses to pay you? To handle this in a professional manner, you must submit an invoice to them and note on it that they are behind in payment. You must let them know they are behind; however many times you decide to let them know is up to you. You might also check with the medical billing organization to which you belong, either at a meeting or in an online forum, to see how this problem is most commonly handled and get advice from other members.

Once a client has ignored his or her overdue invoices, set up an appointment with the doctor so you can meet with him or her in person. Ask why you have not been getting paid. Maybe the client is embarrassed he or she has neglected to pay you, or cannot find the time to pay you. Whatever the issue is, you need to make the client well-aware that you cannot continue like this. Once you have a face-to-face appointment with them and they still have not paid after however long you have given them to pay, then unfortunately you are going to have to contact your lawyer or turn to a collection agency to obtain your payment. From there, it will be out of your hands; hopefully, you will receive payment quickly.

If you decide to take on a certain client and he or she has more than one practice, you will more than likely be responsible for all the practice's locations. You will be responsible for keeping track of patients, making deposits for your clients at their banks if you are working in their office, and checking and calling for accounts that are delinquent.

Below is a sample fees for service form. When a doctor asks what you charge for a certain service, you will be able to hand them the form below. You should charge according to what you have found in your research or what the members of your professional MIB organization have determined to be the going rates. You can choose to add anything you will be offering for services and adjust the prices accordingly.

Sample fee for service form

Fee chart for Mountainside Medical Billing for 2010

Set-up fee for account . . . .$400 monthly
Keeping patients updated monthly . . . .$40 monthly
Electronic claims transmissions . . . .$2 (varies)
Paper claims transmissions . . . .$5 (varies)
Reports . . . . $2 each

Assessing Clients' Needs

Always remember that your clients are the most important part of your business. Your clients are the reason you have a business, and if you are doing your job properly, they are the reason you have income. Every now and then, you will want to ask your customers how they are doing and if they are happy with your business.

You can do client surveys to see what you can do better or how you are measuring up with them. You can also hold meetings to make sure your clients are happy with your business and services. Make sure you are assessing clients' needs on a regular basis. Below are some steps you can take to see how content your clients are with the services you are providing them:

1. Point out to the clients what services you would like to review, if not all of them.

2. Let clients know you would like to evaluate them, asking basically how your company is working out for them.

3. Arrange an appointment for an evaluation with a client.

4. Prepare for client's interview; evaluate each and every one of your clients if you feel the need to do so.

5. Write down what you would like to review with them.

6. Go to the interview, ask the questions that you need, and make sure they are happy with your company; the goal here is to make sure everyone is happy.

The following page has an example of a form you can use to keep track of your clients' satisfaction with your service:

Sample client assessment survey

Mountainside Medical Billing — **Client assessment survey**

Client name: _____ Date: _____

Reason for review: _____

_____

_____

Services offered to this client:

_____

_____

_____

_____

What the client would like to see changed:

_____

_____

What the client would like to see added:

_____

_____

On a scale of 1 to 10, with 10 being excellent service, how would you rate our company?

1   2   3   4   5   6   7   8   9   10

Additional comments:

_____

_____

_____

_____

You want to keep the interview short and make sure you have accomplished what you set out to do. If your clients are unhappy with any of the service you provide for them, it will be time to figure out how to make them happy again and keep their business.

Handling Complaints

There will be times that complaints will arise about your business. Complaints can come from inside your business (from employees) or from outside your business (insurance companies, clients, and anyone who has or does business with your medical billing company). A complaint could arise from anyone at any time. When someone has a complaint and comes to you, you must give them your full attention. If the complaint is about an employee, you need to assure the person who is making the complaint that you will handle it immediately.

You cannot please everyone, so someone at some point will have an issue with you or your business. Do not take the complaints to heart; however, do learn from them, as this is a way to correct any issues within your business. When complaints are made, you must handle them in a professional way. When you are dealing with clients, patients, and others, you must be 100 percent positive at all times. You do not want to get too many complaints, as this will affect your business.

To help keep everyone happy, you must let all your clients know the following:

- They are important to your business.

- You are happy to serve them.

- You will go out of your way to make them happy.

- You will fulfill their needs.

- You are here to take care of them.

After your client base has grown, you may want to expand your business and hire employees. Hopefully, over the course of your medical billing career, you will have such a large client base that you will need to hire several employees to handle all the work that your business will have.

Chapter 12

Expanding Your Business and Hiring Staff

When your medical billing business grows, you may want to hire staff. If you have decided on hiring employees, you will need to advertise for help and make appointments for interviews. Be patient, as it may take some time for you to find an employee who is well-qualified to work in your medical billing business.

You may choose, especially at first, to manage your medical billing business operations by yourself. At some point, you may make the decision to hire a manager to oversee daily operations and staff while you attend to other duties involved in your business. But if you hire a manager, here are a few things you need to know about a successful manager.

A successful manager is someone who leads by example and provides recognition for employees who do likewise. He or she also helps people grow and develop their capabilities and skills through education and on-the-job training. A successful manager enables staff to collaborate more effectively with each other. He or she communicates with employees and clients effectively, not only by print and e-mail, but in person with strong listening skills and the ability to provide feedback. An effective and successful manager also builds responsible and effective interpersonal relationships. He or she knows how to develop a work environment that facilitates positive morale and recognition. A successful manager understands and recognizes the financial aspects of the medical billing business and establishes steps and goals for the business to succeed, and documents staff progress and success in the business as well.

Hiring Employees

The first step in adding employees to your company is determining what qualities you will look for in a potential employee. Your potential employees must be organized and act professionally on your behalf and the business's behalf. They will be speaking with clients, potential clients, and other professionals who are contacting your business. What your employees choose to do will reflect on your business, so choose them carefully.

You also need to consider how easy a potential employee will be to train. Some people do not take direction well, and some do not enjoy working online or with computers; you want to avoid hiring someone like this to work for your company. Someone with experience in accounting or banking would probably be a good match for a medical billing position, considering they have been trained to pay attention to detail and account for every penny. Data entry, nursing, or medical assisting are all job backgrounds that will provide potential employees with some knowledge of computers, what medical billing involves, and medical terminology.

When looking for potential employees, check with your local community college for potential employees, especially if it offers medical billing or medical assisting certification and training. These students are learning the skills you need in your business and are a great potential source of employees, even before they graduate. You can also place a "Help Wanted" ad in your local newspaper or post an advertisement on your Web site or on a job site.

Make sure you are as detailed as possible when writing the description for the type of employees you are looking for. Potential employees should be able to do the following:

- Perform data entry
- Use a multi-line phone system

- Provide efficient customer service

- Retain knowledge of medical billing and coding

- Operate a computer

- Follow directions completely

- Work independently

- Know medical terminology

- Know how to operate a fax machine

- Be at work on time

- Have reliable transportation

- Be prepared to work

- Be well-groomed

Your hiring process should align potential employees with your needs; for example, if you need an accountant, hire an accountant. You are the only one who knows where you need the most help, so make sure you thoroughly examine your company's needs before looking for an employee.

Another option when looking for potential employees is to hire employees through an employment service that has prescreened and interviewed the candidates already. After they have performed the interviews, this service will then send any qualified candidates on to you. Should you decide to utilize these services, you will have to enter into a contractual agreement with the employment service and pay them for their work. This can ultimately save you a lot of time and energy, so it may be worth the investment. The contract lengths vary, along with costs, depending on the job you are hiring for, work skills your employees are required to have, and your geographic location. Many employment agencies provide several types of services, including temporary employees (which might be an option for your business).

Another option is to hire temporary employees through an employment agency that specializes in temps. While a medical billing business is not a seasonal operation, you may need help for a few months while an employee is recovering from surgery or because you feel overwhelmed at the moment with all of your business and home commitments. Maybe you need help over the summer months because you want to take a vacation. There are all kinds of reasons why businesses employ temps, and if you can afford to do so, take advantage of it and get the help you need. Going through a temp agency can save you time, energy, and frustration, and you should end up with someone who is familiar with the business and able to jump into work as soon as he or she is hired.

If you do not want to go through the entire hiring process, which is a long process if you do it accurately and legally, you also have the option of subcontracting your work out to other medical billing professionals if you need some assistance handling all your claims. You might be able to work out an arrangement with another local medical billing company, or you can search online for one that provides this service. You will want to have your attorney draw up a contract for any subcontracting arrangement.

Once you have decided to start interviewing applicants, you must get an interview process together. Consider whether you want someone else to do the interviewing or whether you want to do the interviewing yourself. After you have received interest for your open position, you should have your prospective employees fill out an application and submit their résumés. *You can use the sample job application provided in the accompanying CD-ROM as a guide for what your potential employees can fill out.*

After you have reviewed the completed applications and have selected some candidates, you will want to begin interviewing to find your new employee or employees. The interview process usually follows the format: 1. Call the selected applicant and make an appointment for a job interview. 2. The applicant will answer any and all questions during the interview. Some sample questions may include:

1. Where did you last work?

2. What were your job responsibilities there?

3. Why did you leave?

4. What kind of a job are you looking for?

5. Why does this job interest you?

6. What are your medical billing certifications or credentials?

7. Did you take classes or a course in medical billing? If so, where and when?

8. How do you feel about re-certifying and taking classes to do so?

9. What do you like most about medical billing?

10. How does HIPAA affect your job as a medical insurance biller?

11. Can you appeal every denial that I get from the insurance company for me? (Since you can only appeal the improperly denied claims, an experienced biller knows the answer is no.)

12. How do you think you can contribute positively to our company?

Testing prospective employees

After you have interviewed a candidate, you may want to test them based on skills related to the position for which he or she is applying (basic math, or perhaps some simple coding or claims filing questions). Here are some sample tests you can have your prospective employees perform:

- Write down the word descriptions of five medical procedures and ask them to find the correct codes.

- Provide, on paper, five illness/symptoms/diagnosis and have them find the right ICD-10 code. For example, if you wrote "maxillary sinusitis," then the applicant should know enough to ask to look at the chart to find out if this is acute or chronic. Applicants should not just select the first code they find without seeing if they need to find the fourth or fifth digit of the ICD-10 code to be complete. Do not hire anyone who is obviously guessing. If you see applicants choosing the code from the index without consulting the numerical section to read more about the code and the choices available, you do not want to hire them.

After the applicant passes the medical billing test, have him or her do the following:

- Provide all background documents required (for certification, licensing, education, and so on).

- Take a drug screening test (the results should be sent to you). This is not mandatory but you will probably feel better knowing that your new employee has passed a drug screen.

- Obtain a felony screening on the applicants who are qualified to do the job and whom you want to hire.

- Discuss with you or your office manager what positions are open, the pay rate, and hours, and make sure the applicant is agreeable with them.

- After being hired, the applicant will attend any orientation session or receive "on the job" training.

Negligent hiring

One thing you must be aware of when hiring employees is the danger of negligent hiring. Negligent hiring is when an employer fails to exercise reasonable caution when hiring an employee. If an employee causes harm to a client, customer, or another employee and the employer should have known that the individual was a risk to hire, the courts have found the companies liable and can require them to pay the plaintiff. Employers in negligent hiring cases end up paying thousands of dollars and lose more than 70 percent of lawsuits.

Employers should protect themselves from negligent hiring by verifying all pertinent information about each job applicant and by completely checking references before making a job offer. A criminal records search should also be conducted for each place of residence a candidate has lived at for at least the last seven years. Employers should contact at least three business references with whom the applicant has actually worked on a daily basis over the last seven years. In addition, employers should also confirm all licenses and degrees listed by the applicant. Every employer should be able to show that reasonable care was used in the hiring process by taking these simple steps. In order to avoiding negligent hiring liability, the employer must show that he or she did not neglect their responsibility to properly screen employees. A thorough background check on a new employee usually costs less than a new employee's first day of work.

Once the applicant has passed the interview, drug screening, and felony screening, and he or she has been offered a position, orientation is the next step. This is where your new hire fills out all paperwork, tax forms, and goes through the training process. The paperwork that must be filled out includes the W-4 form so that you (the employer) will know how much to withhold from the employee's paycheck for federal income taxes; an I-9 form, which provides documentation that the new hire is authorized to work in the United States; the state W-4 form; and state and local tax documents (which you can obtain from your state's Web site). The alternative to a formal orientation is to merely start the new hire and let him or her learn by doing; "on the job" training, so to speak.

Training Your Employees to Serve Clients

When hiring employees, you must ensure they are properly trained to serve your clients. If your employees are not trained properly, your business could deteriorate, but when employees are fully prepared, things tend to run more efficiently. You should hire employees according to your policies and procedures, drug testing, and hiring skills. They should then undergo some formal training or orientation for one to two weeks. Show them everything they need to know, including answering the phones, submitting claims, talking to clients, and properly representing your business. You must remember that whomever you hire is reflecting upon your business.

Soft skills

Soft skills are otherwise known as people skills, and they are sometimes hard to learn. Soft skills are skills you need to acquire to train your employees correctly. They cover a variety of skills that influence how people interact with each other. Soft skills include:

- Leadership

- Problem solving

- Team building

- Listening skills

- Effective communication

- Analytical thinking

- Creativity

- Flexibility

There are plenty of online resources to research and contact, such as the two listed below, to help you learn soft skills effectively in order to train your employees correctly.

Soft Skills Courseware: www.softskillscourseware.com — This company offers training material in a flexible, unique solution. You can purchase an individual course title or the whole training library. Courses available include "Building Self Esteem and Assertiveness Skills," "Conflict Resolution: Dealing with Difficult People," and "Motivation Training: Motivating Your Workforce."

Business Training Library: www.bizlibrary.com — The Business Training Library offers more than 3,500 Web-based training courses, with new course titles added every month. Some course titles to choose from are "Business Interpersonal Communication Skills Simulation," "Developing

Employees," "Addressing Problem Performance," and "Communicating to Get Results."

These companies, as well as several others you can find online, offer the correct way to train your employees, correctly manage your business, and manage a company with employees and a human resources department. They are an easy way to get the training you need from the comfort of your office.

After you train your employees, you will need to consider what kind of insurance you will offer them. It is customary to offer your employees health insurance after offering them a position with your company.

Insurance Options

You should research the cost of offering employees medical insurance, such as health, dental, and vision. If these are all too expensive, look at offering them basic medical/health insurance (which usually covers doctors' visits, prescriptions, or hospitalization), or even catastrophic medical insurance, which is insurance with a high deductible that will be useful if an employee is in an auto accident or comes down with a life-threatening disease. Check with a trusted insurance agent, and ask him or her to suggest a few different low-cost policies you can offer your employees.

If you hire a medical insurance billing professional, it would be advisable to get errors and omissions (E&O) insurance. This insurance is similar to malpractice insurance because it covers your business in case a client should sue you. (Do not forget that your insurance costs are deductible as legitimate business expenses.) Let your insurance agent know you are interested in obtaining insurance coverage to protect your business from areas such as liability, flood, fire, and physical injury.

When you hire employees, you must have workers' compensation insurance. Workers' compensation is useful in case something happens to one of your employees, such as getting burnt by the hot water in your office or falling down the stairs. This insurance protects employers from lawsuits from workplace injuries and disabilities that could put them out of business if they were sued by an injured/disabled employee. Even if your office is in your home and your employees work there, your homeowner's insurance will likely not pay for any accident claims because they will probably say it is a workers' compensation case. Workers' comp varies by state, so an insurance agent will be able to discuss what is required where your business is located. Your insurance agent will no doubt bring up this valuable coverage with you.

After your new employee has had a few weeks' experience working with your company, you may want to consider evaluating his or her work performance to ensure it is up to your business's standards. It is a good idea to have new employees undergo training for about two weeks and have an evaluation at the end of their first 30 days of employment.

Employee Evaluations

This evaluation will show you how much the employee has grown in his or her job performance, or it will show you whether he or she will be a good fit for your business. You will need to let your employees know after they are hired they will be in training for two weeks. You should also let the new employee know he or she will undergo a job performance evaluation in 30 days. The following page has a performance evaluation you can use or change to help you assess your employees at the end of their evaluation period.

Sample employee evaluation form

Your business's name here

Employee's name: _____

Employee's hiring date: _____

Today's date: _____

Has employee made it to work on time every day?. . . . . Yes No

Has employee been prepared for work?. Yes No

Has employee done the work he or she was hired to do?. . . . . Yes No

Is employee's job performance satisfactory?. . . . . Yes No

Is the employee polite and courteous to others? . . . . Yes No

Does the employee have good communication skills? . . . . Yes No

Does the employee follow guidelines, rules, and regulations?. . . . . . Yes No

Does employee work well with others? . . . . Yes No

Does the employee take direction well?. Yes No

Employee's strengths:

_____

_____

_____

Employee's weaknesses:

_____

_____

_____

Comments:

_____

_____

_____

_____

Employee is retained and will be revaluated in six months. . . . . Yes No

Employee will be re-evaluated in 30 days. . . . . Yes No

Employee will be terminated. . . . . Yes No

Management signature _____ Date _____

Employee signature _____ Date _____

The evaluation form can be changed or copied to suit your business's needs. Make sure the evaluation is positive and most of the questions are answered with a yes. If most of the questions are answered with a no, you may want to consider firing the employee. If the answers consist of equal amounts of yes and no's, try re-evaluating the employee again in 30 days to see if anything has improved. If you answered all questions with a yes, the employee may be just what you need in your business.

When managing your employees, you will be responsible for making sure they understand their job. They should have a manual about the company's rules, regulations, policies, and procedures. They should be well-aware when they report for work in the morning what their job for the day is, what they need to accomplish, and when their breaks will occur. You are responsible for making sure they have all the information they need to know. If they have any problems or issues, they should report to the supervisor, depending on whether you have hired a supervisor other than yourself to look after the employees and to deal with such issues when it comes to the employees. If the employee is not happy with the supervisor, it is highly advisable for him or her to bring it to your attention. If your employees feel they are not being treated fairly, they may leave your business. You need to respect your employees and treat them as you would want to be treated. If, after you hire an employee and evaluate him or her, he or she is not living up to your expectations — and you do not think his or her work will improve over time — you may want to consider releasing that person from your business.

Firing Employees

If you hire employees and they fail to live up to your expectations, then it is time to give them a warning. Your warning can be verbal, or you may choose to keep a paper record of the warning to store in the employee's file. You can give your employees a warning for the following:

- Being late

- Being rude to a client

- Messing up claims

- Answering the phone unprofessionally

- Spending time on their personal cell phone

- Gossiping about other staff members while at the office

- Disrespecting other staff members

- Not doing the job that they were hired to do

- Improperly handling work situations (for example, trying to handle issues on their own instead of notifying a supervisor)

Here is an example of what a warning may look like:

Employee warning form

Employee's name:_____

Today's date: _____

Reason for the warning:

_____

_____

_____

Warning number: 1   2   3

If an employee is warned three times but the problem behavior still persists, you should considering reprimanding him or her with probation or possibly terminating the employee. Giving a verbal warning first would be the professional way to go. If the employee violates the rules again, he or she should be given a written warning. Once he or she hits his or her third violation, it is time ask the employee for a meeting and let him or her know this is the last warning and the next action will be termination of employment. These matters should be conducted behind closed doors where no one is around to hear you. Do not mention to anyone else what goes on between you and an employee.

After you have employees working for you, you will be responsible for tracking their hours and ensuring they get paid the proper amount. These are two of the most important responsibilities a business owner will have, so it is important you stay on top of this paperwork.

Payroll and Keeping Track of Hours

An idea for how to keep track of employee hours is a time clock, which can be especially helpful if you have several employees with different schedules. A time clock will keep track of their hours, and you will also be able to keep track of how many times they are late.

You may choose to hire a payroll company to track employee work hours and paychecks. This will cost you money, but it will save you time and work, so you will need to decide if it is worth the expense. You might find an individual who is experienced at payroll and can handle the job for you, either part-time or off-site, which is most likely cheaper than paying a payroll company. Make sure this person has excellent references because you will be entrusting him or her with paying your employees and handling your business's money. Either this person will have the necessary payroll software program, or you will have to purchase one for him or her to use (ask for recommendations about the best program to buy).

Below are two examples of national companies that offer online payroll services to businesses. You can also look in your yellow pages to find a local company.

CompuPay^{SM}**: www.compupay.com** — CompuPay processes your payroll, manages your payroll taxes, and enables you to view payroll reports

24 hours a day from any computer with Internet access. CompuPay offers three online payroll options: PowerPayroll, XpressPayroll, and CompuPay PayrollOnline. PowerPayroll is ideal for small businesses, with payroll, direct deposit, and tax filing solutions. XpressPayroll provides cost-effective, streamlined payroll and tax filing solutions. CompuPay PayrollOnline includes human resources, reporting capabilities, and more than 40 standard online payroll reports.

Intuit Payroll: www.paycycle.com — Intuit Online Payroll services are designed for small businesses. Just enter employee hours and pay rate and you can receive paychecks. Click to print them or utilize the company's free employee direct deposit services. Federal, state, and local payroll taxes are automatically withheld, and there is a 30-day free trial to test the software.

Respecting Everyone at Work

Another important responsibility you will have as a business owner is to ensure everything at your office is running smoothly, and this includes interactions between staff members and clients. Everyone involved in your business, such as clients, employees, patients, and even the people from whom you buy furniture, should be treated with respect. Respect should not be regarded as a choice, but rather as a guideline, a policy, and a rule that you and your employees must follow. If your employees choose to be disrespectful, they should be prepared to be disciplined or terminated. If you, as the owner of the company, choose to be disrespectful to fellow employees and clients, then you might as well prepare to have no business. If the business is grounded in disrespect, it will not last long; no one wants to work with disrespectful people. Being respectful means communicating: The business should be open and honest, and all employees should be able to communicate without upsetting anyone. Keeping communication open, honest, and respectful is perhaps the most crucial key to client and employee interaction.

Meetings

When you have staff members within your business, it will be essential to have staff meetings. Your staff meetings will help all employees stay up-to-date with all the informational requirements of the business and what is going on with clients and claims. Use this time to discuss any issues anyone may be having with another employee or with the company itself. Have an agenda of what you hope to accomplish during a particular meeting.

Regular staff meetings can do the following:

- See if employees have any issues they need to discuss.

- Grant rewards for the most claims paid.

- Discuss attendance problems.

- Update everyone on any new information regarding billing and claims processing and filing.

Let everyone know of potential or ongoing issues, like common billing and claims mistakes that are going on, new changes in codes, an upcoming conference that you want them to attend, and workplace problems, like tardiness or too much personal time on the phone.

Most meetings follow this format:

1. Take attendance at every meeting.

2. Provide an agenda for each employee.

3. Review what happened at the last meeting.

4. Answer any questions employees have about the prior meeting.

5. Discuss your reason for this meeting.

6. Answer questions employees may have.

7. Ask if there are any other issues (aside for the ones on the agenda) that need to be discussed.

8. Dismiss the meeting and thank everyone for coming.

Make sure you are prepared for your meetings. Having refreshments would be a treat for your employees, and this gesture would let everyone mingle and become closer. Meetings are one of the best sources of communication. You can schedule a meeting to discuss all the feedback that your clients have provided to help determine what is working, what is not working, and how you can improve what is not working.

Your meetings are a place where everyone can gather and share information, plans, and problems. Meetings are a great way to keep the peace and keep the medical billing business running the way it should. You want your meetings to be energetic and the attendees to be willing to participate and be fully involved. You do not have to go out of your way and spend a large amount of money to make your meetings interesting, fun, and successful; doing something simple like bringing in a snack or coffee can always affect your meetings for the better.

Motivating Workers

Incentives are a great way to motivate your employees. It shows them that work can be enjoyable and that you value their help. Sometimes business owners will get caught up in their own work and just assume employees are there because they have to be. This is not true; employees can go work anywhere they can find a job. If employees do not receive adequate recognition, they may eventually want to find a new job that recognizes and appreciates their contributions and achievements.

An effective way to motivate your employees is to give them an incentive to work harder. Payment by commission, or commission in addition to an hourly pay rate, is often a very effective way to work. For example, if you charge physicians a percentage of what your business collects for them, an employee might be able to earn a commission from the amount he or she was able to collect for each physician.

Different types of incentives you can offer your employees include:

- Attendance awards

- Lunch (out of the office) with the owner

- Dress-down day

- A bonus for whoever brings in the most claims for the week or month

- An extended lunch

- Bring your kids to work day

- A day off

- Employee party

- A small hourly raise

- A certain amount of money for every claim they get paid

Hiring employees can be an exciting yet daunting task. To ensure your business runs smoothly, you need to make sure your employees are a good fit for your organization, just as Greg Barnes did in the following case study.

CASE STUDY: PHYSICIAN SERVICES

Greg Barnes, owner
www.PSMBS.com

I worked for a doctor and made connections with other doctors who needed billing done. I started my own medical billing company in 1991 and purchased business software and supplies. I do not have any medical billing training or certification, just first-hand work experience and a Bachelor of Science degree in business.

This industry has changed in many ways since I began my company: electronic filing of claims; submitting paper claims; following up on claims; posting of payments; handling all incorrectly paid explanations of benefits (EOBs) (an explanation of benefits from the insurance carrier summarizes the details of a claim that has been submitted and the reimbursement); and evaluating doctors' CPT codes and fees to maximize reimbursement.

Today, the biggest change I see is that more claims are being processed electronically, and software is getting more advanced to where payments can be posted electronically instead of by paper.

If you want to open your own medical insurance billing business, first go to work for a doctor and learn billing to see if you like it. If you do, become the best biller that doctor has ever had and tell the doctor that you want to work from home. Then use him or her as a referral to get other clients.

Make sure you add staff and train them when you start to grow. The biggest complaint in this business is poor service. Buying the $6,000- to $8,000-programs where you are trained for three days is a waste of time and money. The classes that you take in college on coding are good but will not train you for the nuts and bolts of billing; that is why I say to go to work for a doctor and experience it live.

My business serves chiropractors. Today I have more than 20 employees who all work from their homes and 120 clients nationwide.

Conclusion

S tarting a new business can be exciting, challenging, time-consuming, and scary. It will not be easy, but it can be done — and the end results can be well worth the hard efforts of making your business succeed. There will be problems that you will experience along the way, but that is common for every business; you will learn more about the medical billing business through trial and error. There will always be help and support from numerous people, books, and Web sites. *See Appendix D at the end of this book for more.*

The best resources come from the people who have already experienced what you are doing. After reading this book, you will be able to use it as a reference. Do not rush into everything; take your time and make sure everything is going as you planned. When you start to resent the business or get tired of it, it is time to refresh yourself. Make sure you follow all rules, regulations, and policies for the IRS, HIPAA, and all the other health care entities alongside which you will be working.

There is much to do, but if you stay on track, opening your own medical billing company can and will be a rewarding experience.

Appendix A

Sample Business Plan

Business plan

Mountainside Medical Billing
5555 Mountainside Ave.
Columbus, Ohio 43232
Contact: Laura Gater
555-555-5555
info@medicalbilling.com
January 19, 2010

Table of contents

Mission statement

We will provide our clients with quality, up-to-date information and help them receive payment in a timely manner by submitting medical claims securely and accurately. We will also offer them the highest quality of customer service.

Executive summary of the business

Medical billing services exist to manage medical practices. Their services alleviate medical professionals of time-consuming, tedious work, but they seldom offer a way to increase the practice's bottom line significantly. Mountainside Medical Billing, however, will take over this time-consuming work and alleviate an overworked medical staff, along with increasing the practice's return from insurance carriers.

According to national statistics, approximately 70 percent of insurance claims are paid by insurance companies. Mountainside Medical Billing can increase the percentage of claims paid to around 98 percent, with the help of electronic claims filing.

Statistics show that turnaround for payment of paper insurance claims is 60 to 120 days, which can cause significant outstanding receivables for the medical practice. Mountainside Medical Billing, with the help of electronic claims filing, can generally have reimbursement in the physician's hand within seven to 14 days. This will significantly diminish outstanding receivables and improve the practice's cash flow.

Thanks to extensive editing conducted on electronic claims prior to their transmission to carriers, medical insurance claims are now submitted with an accuracy rate of 98 percent.

Outstanding receivables grew at a fast rate for many medical practices, and it became routine to write off bad debt. Adequate profit margins, however, enabled medical practices to disregard reliable business procedures. With the advent of managed care organizations into the medical industry, physicians face shrinking profit margins and now realize that they will have to adopt more efficient business practices. Mountainside Medical Billing is prepared to assist local medical providers make the transition to electronic technology that will help promote their business success and ensure quality health care for all.

Mountainside Medical Billing Business is an owner-operated business located in Columbus, Ohio, serving local and nationwide clients. This company will use honest work ethics to provide medical billing services to our clients and help our clients achieve their business goals. We will offer accounts receivable, claims submitting, and account collections services. We have found the need for a medical billing office in our local area after carefully evaluating physician practices and realizing the demand for quality medical billing services and decreased claims rejections.

We have already signed an agreement with the owners of Mountainside Office Building to lease a 2,500-square-foot office for two years. This office is conveniently located in the Columbus Medical Complex. Presently, the owner and operator of Mountainside Medical Billing will focus on finding clients for this business and will focus on delivering services that prospective clients greatly need. Our goal is to find clients within our community, offer them honest services, and deliver services within a timely manner. All of our services will help physicians focus on their practice, leaving all the patient accounts to Mountainside Medical Billing. We plan to research potential clients and their principal needs; once we know this information, we will offer the potential clients more services if they are within our scope of business. The objective for this business plan is to request a $50,000 line of credit from your bank.

Business description

Mountainside Medical Billing will provide our clients with error-free claims submission, making claims easily and more quickly paid. We offer convenient ways for our clients to locate us. They can access our Web site 24 hours a day, seven days a week, and we can be easily contacted via cell phone and voicemail. We will keep clients current with all medical billing codes, policies, and regulations. We will evaluate each client's superbill to verify that all codes are correct and determine which of our services would benefit them the most. Mountainside Medical Billing plans to achieve its goal of assuming more medical billing clients by giving each and every client the same amount of care and attention. Mountainside Medical Billing will offer friendly customer service, give our clients the utmost respect, and focus our full attention on our clients by offering them a full-service medical billing company.

Management and staffing

Ronald Weese, CPC, CMCP, has worked in the medical field for 14 years. He was the office manager for a local medical practice in Columbus, Ohio, and did its medical billing for eight years. He has two assistants (Ashley Jenkins and Marian Turner) to help with marketing and managing the office, such as answering phones, filing, and submitting claims. The three of them at this time feel they can handle all operations of this business successfully.

All of our management team members have acquired formal training in medical billing and are thus familiar with the language and operations of the health care industry. They have also learned how to utilize medical billing software, understand governmental and insurance regulations, and work effectively within the health care community. When we approach potential clients, it is important we are able to understand the specific needs of their practice. Each of the three management team members at Mountainside Medical Billing has become a Certified Medical Claims Professional (CMCP), a new certification issued by the American Career Certification Board (ACCB). This certification shows the potential client that we understand all the regulations and terminology necessary to provide quality services.

As the business of Mountainside Medical Billing increases, we hope to add two more billers with at least a CMCP certification. We hope to have the need for one biller within 12 months and for a second biller within 18 months, if the projections outlined in this proposal are accurate.

Marketing/industry analysis

Americans spent more than $2 trillion on health care in 2007 (Entrepreneur Press and Jennifer Dorsey), and the numbers continue to rise. The health care industry provides 14 million jobs, and it is estimated that the industry will generate 3.2 million new jobs by 2018. In today's health care industry, for any provider to have a successful practice he or she must get paid. Without medical billing services, doctors have a hard time getting paid. It is almost impossible for the average doctor to stay up-to-date on the number of ever-expanding insurance companies, each with its own particular guidelines, as well as take care of the needs of his or her patients. Medical billing specialists handle the administrative and accounting requirements needed to help the provider earn his or her living.

Before Medical Insurance Billers (MIBs) were around, patients had to submit their own claims, but this is not the case today. Today, electronic filing is advantageous because you get paid faster and there are fewer errors. Once they diagnose the patient and determine treatment, the doctor will check the appropriate box with the diagnosis code, which tells the MIB what to bill for. Health care providers use a series of common codes for procedures, called Current Procedural Terminology (CPT) codes. The codes are published by the AMA and are updated annually. Although MIBs do not code, they must know the common codes for the common medical procedures they will bill for and understand ways to bill most efficiently for certain procedures.

The insurance industry has grown exponentially, and the vast majority of a provider's income comes from insurance companies. Insurance agencies, Medicare, and Medicaid must guard against fraud and abuse, and all have stringent guidelines to protect their interests. There are many insurance companies in operation today; the number of rules to follow can become overwhelming. Because of these difficulties, the demand for medical billing services has grown. Most medical providers hire a specialist in medical insurance claims billing. Today, it is much more common to file claims electronically, which means the claims processing is faster and more efficient; providers can be paid much faster. With the advent of electronic billing, this has opened a new career trend in virtual work, with medical providers outsourcing their claims to remote (or off-site) medical billing services.

Most medical providers will seek a medical billing specialist with extensive experience in medical billing, coding, and accounts receivable management. Although training is not mandatory, formal training in medical billing or certification in medical coding will give credibility to your services and give you an advantage in obtaining clients.

We have researched our competitors and found only three medical billing practices in the Columbus metropolitan area, which only offer claims submission and are not considered full-service medical billing companies. They have only a few clients because they do not offer more services. There are other competitors available, but they are not within a 50-mile radius. Our company offers more than claims submission; we offer any service the doctor wishes for us to provide, in particular bill collection, past due accounts, accounts receivables, and claim submission. Our competitors are Rainbow Billing (which only offers claims submission), Emerson Billing, and Fifth Avenue Billing (both of which only offer claims submission and do not offer follow-up services on patient accounts that are past due).

Marketing strategy

The areas we have chosen to target for marketing are wealthy neighborhoods where residents have money to go to the doctor. Within those neighborhoods, we will then target medical complexes and clinics that are home to physicians, dentists, and physiologists. We will market to those medical providers who do not have time to handle claims submission, accounts receivable, and accounts collection. We will also market to medical providers having issues staying up-to-date with and submitting claims. The medical field is consistently growing as new doctors graduate every year and new patients are born every day. In addition, the aging baby boomer population means many physicians' offices are being overwhelmed with claims that need to be filed, billed, or paid.

Operations

Mountainside Medical Billing's three employees are considered members of the management team and will handle all duties, from answering the phone to customer service to submitting claims. The owner, Ronald Weese, will focus on all marketing and public relations functions and will most likely not be in the office very much, as he will be visiting prospective clients and attending medical conferences in order to promote the business at trade shows there. Ronald Weese is the head of the management team, and as such, will oversee the office, future employees, and daily aspects of the business.

The new office location will provide one office and enough space for two cubicles for the other two members of the management team, with extra room to grow as new employees are added according to need.

Ashley Jenkins is the office manager. She will answer calls as well as screen and forward e-mails from clients and prospective clients, in addition to handling all the filing, mailing, faxing, and customer service inquiries. Marian Turner's main responsibility is to submit medical claims. Mr. Weese will oversee denied claims and oversee relationships with new clients, along with handling contracts and legal matters. He will review daily reports with the other staff members and assign tasks to them as needed, based on daily claims activity.

Financial projections

Our financial plan consists of our start-up expenses and the operating costs detailed in this plan. Our plan consists of the following:

Start-up expenses

- Registration/licensing fees

- Utility deposits and fees

- Equipment

- Rental/lease deposit

- Software

- Memberships in medical billing organizations and local organizations (Chamber of Commerce and other business organizations)

Operating expenses

- Rent payment

- Utility payments

- Advertising

- Loan payment

- Office equipment payment

- Claim submission fees

- Income statement

- Balance sheet

- Projected cash flow sheet

Currently, utility companies require deposits for their service or at least payment for a month in advance to turn on services. The following is our utility plan:

- Electric: $150 deposit

- Telephone: No deposit required for service, but requires a month in advance, which is $85

- Gas: $200

- Water: $200

- Garbage disposal: We have a trash receptacle in the parking lot, which is part of the office rental, but we are required to pay $100 a month, no deposit required; a month's payment in advance is required

- Fire inspection: $150

- Zoning is commercial

- No permits are needed at this time

- Payroll: For the three executives, approximate payroll will be $25,000 yearly per executive, totaling for $75,000 for 2010. As you can see, we anticipate $50,000 in start-up costs. We will also need the following essential office equipment: a computer with a printer and scanner, a telephone, and a fax machine. We will also need high-speed Internet access and a second phone line

Utility deposits and expenses total: $885

Sample budget sheet for start-up costs:

Rent $1,500
Office supplies $7,000
Insurance $700
CMS forms $35
Software. $4,000
Utilities. $885
Clearinghouse fees $300
Total $14,420

Conclusion

Mountainside Medical Billing will provide clients with error-free claims submission, making claims easily and more quickly paid. The demand for medical billing services has grown. With the advent of electronic billing, this has opened a new career trend in virtual work, with medical providers outsourcing their claims to remote (off-site) medical billing services, like ours. We have evaluated physician practices and realized the demand for quality medical billing services in our area.

The aging baby boomer population means many physicians' offices are being overwhelmed with claims that need to be filed, billed, or paid.

All of our management team members have acquired formal training in medical billing and are thus familiar with the language and operations of the health care industry. They have also learned how to utilize medical billing software, understand governmental and insurance regulations, and work effectively within the health care community.

Clients can access our Web site 24 hours a day, seven days a week, and we can be easily contacted via e-mail, cell phone, and voicemail. We will keep clients current with all medical billing codes, policies, and regulations.

We have researched our competitors and found only three medical billing practices in the Columbus metropolitan area, which only offer claims submission and are not considered full-service medical billing companies. They have only a few clients because they do not offer more services.

Supporting documentation

Attached are résumés of the Mountainside Medical Billing management team, as well as the owner's tax returns and personal financial statements for the last three years. Also attached are copies of the business license, management team certifications, and other relevant legal documents. A copy of the office lease is also attached.

Appendix B

Abbreviations

AAFP (American Academy of Family Physicians): The AAFP, which was founded in 1947, has a mission to improve the health of patients, families, and communities by serving its members' needs professionally and creatively.

AAMC (American Association of Medical Colleges): The AAMC represents 148 medical schools in the United States and Canada, as well as about 400 major teaching hospitals, including 68 Department of Veterans Affairs medical centers and nearly 90 academic and scientific societies.

AAOS (American Academy of Orthopedic Surgeons (also referred to as American Association of Orthopedic Surgeons)): The preeminent provider of musculoskeletal education to orthopedic surgeons and other medical providers in the world.

AAPC (American Academy of Professional Coders): This association was founded in 1988 to educate and certify physician-based medical coders and also aims to elevate the standards of medical coding by offering training, certification, continuing education, job opportunities, and networking.

ACCB (American Career Certification Board): This body creates baseline standards for anyone entering new careers. This organization aims to train those about to enter into a new career in the medical field.

ACP (American College of Physicians): This group that represents physicians across America specializes in preventing, detecting, and treating illnesses. This is the largest medical specialty organization in the country.

ACS (American Cancer Society): This organization is dedicated to eliminating cancer by preventing the disease and diminishing suffering from cancer through research, service, and advocacy.

ACS (American College of Surgeons): This organization provides education and credential programs as well as management services to other associations. It also markets new insurance and investment products.

ADA (American Dental Association): This association aims to unite organizations and people to make a lasting difference through improved dental health.

ADA (American Diabetes Association): ADA funds research to prevent, manage, and cure diabetes and provides objectives and credible information by giving a voice to those who are denied rights because of this disease.

AHIMA (American Health Information Management Association): This group is dedicated to managing personal health information that is required to deliver quality health care to the American public.

AMA (The American Medical Association): The AMA helps doctors assist patients by uniting doctors across the country to work on the most pressing public health and professional issues.

AMBA (American Medical Billing Association): This association was developed so medical billers across the United States could network, share information and ideas, and also support and educate each other.

ASCA (Administrative Simplification Compliance Act): This act prohibits payment for services or supplies that a provider did not bill Medicare for electronically.

ASO (Administrative Services Only): These services are allowed in employee benefit packages and allow more control over the benefit plans.

BBB (Better Business Bureau): This organization sets standards for marketplace trust and encourages best practices by celebrating marketplace role models and denouncing substandard behavior.

BCBSA (BlueCross and BlueShield Association): This is the nation's oldest and largest health insurance provider.

BNI (Beneficiary Notices Initiative): These notices are given by health care providers and communicate financial liability and appeal rights and protection under fee-for-service Medicare and Medicare Advantage.

CAHIIM (Committee on Accreditation for Health Informatics & Information Management Education): This organization accredits Health Information Management education programs at the master's, baccalaureate, and associate's level.

CAP (Claims Assistance Professional): These professionals assist people with denied claims, filing claims, and more.

CBMCS (Certified Basic Medical Coding Specialist): This is a person who is certified to change the description of a medical diagnosis and process into the correct code.

CCA (Certified Coding Associate): This represents the most basic level of credentials one can receive from the American Health Information Management Association.

CCAP (Certified Claims Assistance Professional): A person certified for assisting people with medical claims.

CCS (Certified Coding Specialist): Someone who works typically in a hospital setting who is skilled in classifying medical data from patients' records.

CCS-P (Certified Coding Specialist – Physician-based): Coding practitioners who specialize in physician-based settings.

CECP (Certified Electronic Claims Professional): This person provides the electronic administrative link between the small- or medium-sized physician health care facilities with the major health care insurers. This person enters information about the patient and sends it to the correct health care payer.

CEU (Continuing Education Unit): A unit of measurement used in continuing education that is required for a professional to keep his or her license valid.

CHBME (Certified Health Care Billing & Management Executive): This is the only association that represents third-party medical billers.

CHDA (Certified Health Data Analyst): A health data analysts who has taken an exam that requires him or her to acquire, manage, interpret, analyze, and transform data into information while balancing the strategic vision with daily details.

CHPS (Certification in Health Care Privacy & Security): A certification the American Health Information Management Associate gives to qualify someone to know how to implement, design, and administer security and privacy protection programs in health care organizations.

CMBA (Certified Medical Billing Associate): The main goal of this association is to provide members with information dealing with medical billing and other related topics that will help develop new skills through enhancing knowledge.

CMCP (Certified Medical Claims Professional): A person certified in medical coding or someone who has become certified in changing descriptions of medical diagnoses and procedures into universal medical code numbers.

CMN (Certificate of Medical Necessity): A form required by the Centers for Medicare and Medicaid Services to claim an item of durable medical equipment; is medically necessary for a Medicare beneficiary.

CMP (Competitive Medical Plan): A health care plan other than an HMO that meets the standard for a Medicare risk-sharing contract.

CMS (Centers for Medicare and Medicaid Services): A federal agency that is within the U.S. Department of Health and Human Services that controls the Medicare program. CMS also works with the state governments to administer Medicaid and State Children's Health Insurance program.

CMSCS (Certified Multi-Specialty Coding Specialist): A coding specialist certified by AHIMA that certifies in-depth knowledge of all major coding systems, health information documentation, and numeric code-assigning to each procedure and diagnosis.

CNS (Central Nervous System): Part of the nervous system that functions to coordinate all the activities within the body.

COLD (Chronic Obstructive Lung Disease): Any medical disorder that disrupts air flow.

CPC-H (Certified Professional Coder-Outpatient Hospital): Someone certified in assigning codes for diagnoses and services performed in an outpatient setting.

CPC-P (Certified Professional Coder-Payer): This certification shows a person is proficient in coding guidelines and reimbursement for all services from the payer's perspective.

CPT (Current Procedural Terminology): A systematic listing and coding of procedures and services a physician would provide.

DME (Durable Medical Equipment): Any medical equipment used at home to help improve a patient's quality of life.

DMERC (Durable Medical Equipment Regional Carrier): A Medicare contractor who is responsible for administering durable medical equipment benefits for a region.

DRG (Diagnosis-Related Group): A sorting system that places hospitals into one of 500 groups.

ECP (Electronic Claims Professional): A person who specialized in electronic claims.

ECS (Electronic Claims Submission): An advanced form of business-to-business communication that links computer systems.

EDI (Electronic Data Interchange): An electronic transmission between two transmissions.

EGHP (Employer Group Health Plan): A health care plan provided by an employer that is fully or partially paid.

EIN (Employer Identification Number): A number issued to avoid anyone who has pay-withholding taxes on employees. It is similar to a corporate social security number.

EMC (Electronic Media Claims): An electronic claim that is entered into a computer and transferred to a system rather than with a claims card. This method is more cost-effective and efficient.

EOB (Explanation of Benefits): An explanation of benefits an insurer provides.

EOMB (Explanation of Medicare Benefits): An explanation of the four different types of

Medicare plants (Part A, Part B, Part C, and Part D).

EPO (Exclusive Provider Organization): An individual care provider or groups of medical care providers that enter a contract with an insurer to provide services to the insurer's clients.

EPSDT (Early and Periodic Screening, Diagnosis, and Treatment): A procedure for children that Medicaid performs, required by every state. This procedure is meant to improve the health of low-income children so they all receive adequate pediatric services.

FECA (Federal Employees Compensation Act): This program provides compensation for federal employees' work-related injuries or illnesses. If the injury resolves in death, compensation is provided to a surviving dependent.

FEHBP (Federal Employee Health Benefits Program): A system of employee health

benefits provided to full-time permanent civilian government employees and qualified U.S. government employees.

FEP (Federal Employee Program): A government-wide service benefit plan that BlueCross BlueShield Association provides; this is part of the Federal Employee Health Benefit Plan.

FERS (Federal Employees Retirement System): A system for federal employees who have worked for five years or more; the employees receive a defined benefit plan, social security, and the thrift savings plan.

FI (Fiscal Intermediary): A private company that contracts with Medicare to pay for some of Part A's bills and some of Part B's bills.

GP (General Practitioner): A physician who mainly focuses on family medicine, treating and preventing illnesses.

HCFA (Health Care Financing Administration): This organization seeks to create a health care system that provides affordable, comprehensive, culturally competent, and high-quality care and consumer education for all people.

HCPCS (HCFA Common Procedure Coding System): Based on CPT codes; used to describe specific items and tasks provided in the delivery of health care.

HIPAA (Health Insurance Portability and Accountability Act of 1996): This act was established primarily to improve the portability of health insurance coverage; it created a set of standards for how health data should be transmitted.

HMO (Health Maintenance Organization): A type of managed care organization where health care coverage is used at hospitals, doctors' offices, and other places the organization contracts with.

ICD-10 (International Classification of Diseases): A classification of coding many health care providers use that the World Health Organization established.

IPA (Independent Practice Association): An organization for independent physicians who contract with managed care organizations; the fees for these services may be negotiated.

MAB (Medical Association of Billers): This organization aims to provide medical billers and coding professionals with resources for diagnostic and procedural coding. This group also offers training and education in a variety of medical billing subjects.

MCS (Managed Care System): A system of health care that controls cost of service, measures the performance of care providers, and manages how services are used. Some examples include Health Maintenance Organizations (HMOs) or Preferred Provider Organization (PPO).

MG (Medigap): Private insurance meant to supplement the expenses Medicare does not pay.

MPP (Minimum Premium Plan): The smallest premium an insurer will write a policy for.

MSO (Managed Service Organization): A medical practice where physicians have more control than in regular practices.

NACAP (National Association of Claims Assistance Professionals, Inc.): A nonprofit organization that provides a directory of claim assistance and focuses on member education.

NCRA (National Cancer Registrars Association): This organization focuses on educating and certifying its members to ensure they have the required knowledge to be superior in their field.

NON-PAR (Non-Participating Physician): A physician who does not accept an insurance provider.

NPI (National Provider Identifier): A ten-digit number unique to each individual that health care providers use for billing purposes. This number must be shared with other providers, clearinghouses, and health plans.

OCR (Optical Character Recognition): A way of converting handwritten or printed text into an electronic file; scanners are able to have this capability.

OIG (Office of the Inspector General): The mission of this organization is to protect the integrity of the Department of Health and Human Services programs, as well as the welfare and health of the programs' beneficiaries.

PAHCOM (Professional Association of Health Care Office Managers): An association providing training to medical office management to help a physician's office run efficiently.

PAHCS (Professional Association of Healthcare Coding Specialists): A network dedicated to enhancing compliance, reimbursement capabilities, and documentation for health care coders.

PAR (Participating Physician): A physician who has a contract with an insurance company and offers to provide services to anyone an insurer covers. The insurer may require a copayment.

PCP (Primary Care Physician): A physician who provides continuing care for a wide range of medical conditions.

POS (Point-of-Service): A type of health care plan that combines the characteristics of HMOs and PPOs; usually has very low deductible and limited co-payments.

PPG (Physician Provider Group): A type of managed health care insurance that has the characteristics of an HMO and a PPO but without the choice of which system to use.

PPO (Preferred Provider Organization): A group of doctors, health care providers, and hospitals that have joined with an insurance company or a third-party administrator to provide health care to clients at a reduced rate.

RHIA (Registered Health Information Administrator): This person acts as a link between health care providers, payers, and patients. They are experts in managing patient information and medical records; they have comprehensive knowledge in medical, ethical, legal, and administrative requirements, as well as the standards related to health care delivery and privacy-protected patient information.

RHIT (Registered Health Information Technician): Professionals who ensure quality medical records by verifying the records are complete; these technicians also use computer applications to analyze patient data and often specialize in coding, diagnosis, and procedures in patient records for reimbursement and research.

RVU (Relative Value Unit): A way to measure the number of resources needed to do services between single and multiple departments used in hospitals.

SBA (Small Business Administration): This is an independent agency that aids, counsels, and protects the interests of small business concerns; preserves free competitive enterprise; and maintains and strengthens the overall economy.

SMI (Supplementary Medical Insurance): Part of the Medicare program where additional coverage is available on a voluntary basis.

SP (Secondary Payer): An insurance plan that pays for services only after a primary insurance plan has made claim or a payment.

TPA (Third-Party Administrator): An organization that processes insurance claims or certain aspects of employee benefit plans for a separate entity.

UCR (Usual, Customary, and Reasonable): A calculation for a managed health care plan of what the plan believes is the appropriate fee to pay for a specific health care product or service.

WHO (World Health Organization): This organization is the directing and coordinating authority for health with the United Nations. WHO is responsible for providing leadership on global health matters, shaping the health research agenda, setting standards, articulating policy options, providing technical support to countries, and assessing and monitoring health trends.

Appendix C

Resource Directory

Below is a list of companies, books, Web sites, and more to help on your journey to a successful business.

Online Resources

American Dental Association: www.ada.org — This site provides learning tools, a list of products the ADA recommends, and information to help providers give the best possible patient care.

American Medical Association: www.ama-assn.org — This organization represents the largest association of physicians and medical students whose mission is to promote the improvement of public health, advance the interest of physicians and their patients, lobby for legislation, and raise money for medical education.

BlueCross and BlueShield Association: www.bcbs.com — One of the nation's oldest and largest groups of health benefits, this group is broken down into 39 individual companies; more than 90 percent of hospitals and more than 80 percent of physicians nationwide accept this plan.

Centers for Medicare and Medicaid Services: www.cms.hhs.gov/default.asp — These programs were enacted to provide health care services to lower-income families.

Department of Health and Human Services: www.hhs.gov — A government program that includes more than 300 programs that specialize in providing essential human services.

HIPAA Comply: www.hipaacomply.com — A Web site that is current with information concerning HIPAA security and privacy compliance.

Medical Association of Billers: www.physicianswebsites.com — The main purpose of this organization is to provide medical billing and coding professionals with a resource for procedural and diagnostic coding. This group also offers education and training in a variety of medical coding and billing subjects.

Medicare: www.medicare.gov — The official Medicare Web site; you can access policy information and anything else related to Medicare.

Sunrise: www.sunrize.com — This site provides billing and collection services to physicians regardless of how large their practice.

Trademark Electronic Application System: www.uspto.gov/teas/index. html — This site is used to register trademarks or service marks.

Unicor Medical Inc.: www.unicormed.com: — A private coding software developer and coding publisher.

U.S. Department of Health and Human Services: www.hhs.gov — The U.S. government's principal agency for protecting the health of all Americans.

U.S. Patent and Trademark Office: www.uspto.gov/web/offices/tac/ tmfaq.htm#Basic — This site is where you would go to find information about trademarks or other service marks; this is especially helpful when you want to check to see if a name you want to use in business has already been trademarked and is being used by another company.

Book Resources:

AMA Health Care Common Procedure Coding System (HCPCS) 2009 Level II, Prentice Hall, 2008.

CPT 2009 Professional Edition, American Medical Association, Prentice Hall.

The Basics of Medical Billing, by Alice Scott and Michele Redmond, Solutions Medical Billing, Inc., 2008.

The Guerrilla Marketing Handbook, by Seth Godin and Jay Conrad Levinson, Mariner Books, 1994.

How to Complete a CMS 1500 Completely and Correctly – Line By Line, Box by Box, by Alice Scott and Michele Redmond, Solutions Medical Billing, Inc., 2007.

Insurance Handbook for the Medical Office, by Marilyn Fordney, Saunders, 2007.

International Classification of Diseases Tenth Edition, Clinical Modification (ICD-10-CM), World Health Organization.

Medical Terminology Demystified, by Dale Layman, McGraw-Hill Professional, 2005.

More Success in Marketing and Management, by Merlin B. Coslick, Electronic Billing Network of America, 1999.

Principles & Practice Of ICD-10 Coding, by Dhirendra Verma & Ali Mohamed El-Sayed, Rochak Publishing, 2008.

UB04 Forms – How to Complete a UB04 Form Completely and Correctly — Line By Line, Box by Box, by Alice Scott and Michele Redmond, CreateSpace, 2007.

The Ultimate Small Business Advisor, by Andi Axman, Entrepreneur Press, 2007.

Understanding Health Insurance, A Guide to Professional Billing, by Joann C. Rowell, Delmar Publishing, 2003.

Appendix D

Insurance Directory (For Business Insurance)

Acceptance Insurance Companies, Inc.
www.aicins.com

Aetna
www.aetna.com

American Family Insurance
www.amfam.com

Assurant Group
www.assurant.com

BlueCross BlueShield Association
www.bcbs.com

CIGNA
www.cigna.com

The Co-operators
www.cooperators.ca

Country Insurance & Financial Services
www.countryfinancial.com

Farmers Insurance Group
www.farmersinsurance.com

Great American Insurance Company
www.greatamericaninsurance.com

GuideOne Insurance
www.guideone.com

Hammond National Insurance Company
www.hammondnational.com

Liberty Mutual Group
www.libertymutual.com

The Mutual of Omaha Company Service
www.mutualofomaha.com

Pekin Insurance Group
www.pekininsurance.com

SAFECO
www.safeco.com

Sentry Insurance
www.sentry.com

State Farm Insurance
www.statefarm.com

UnitedHealthcare
www.uhc.com

Glossary

A

Accept Assignment: Provider accepts Medicare's fees for his/her medical services.

Accounts Receivable (A/R): An accounting transaction that has to do with a business billing and collecting money owed from customers, clients, and so on.

Administrator: The insurance company that writes the insurance policy; also known as the insurer.

Allowed Amount: The dollar amount of a health care provider's bill that an insurance company will pay for a medical procedure or service.

Annual Maximum: Total amount a policy will pay per year.

Appeal: A procedure used to contest a medical claim that has been denied.

Applicant: Person who is applying for insurance coverage.

Assignment: Agreement that assigns a physician the right to receive payment from a patient's insurance company.

Assignment of Benefits: Agreement that directs the insurance carrier to pay benefits to the physician.

Authorized Provider: A doctor who has been authorized by TRICARE to provide medical care and supplies.

B

Basic Plan: An insurance plan that covers basic health care expenditures.

Beneficiary: Person qualified to obtain benefits under an insurance policy (also known as the patient).

Birthday Rule: Multiple-dependent insurance coverage, determined by parents' birth dates.

C

Capitated Payment: A fee that is paid yearly by insurers to doctors, networks or hospitals for providing health care to a patient.

Carrier: An insurance company that provides insurance coverage.

Certified Claims Assistance Professional (CCAP): Certification achieved by passing an examination given by the National Association of Claims Assistance Professionals.

Certified Coding Specialist (CCP): Certification achieved by passing an examination administered by the American Health Information Management Association.

Certified Electronic Claims Professional (CECP): Certification achieved by passing an examination administered by the National Association of Claims Assistance Professionals, Inc.

Certified Electronic Medical Biller (CEMB): Certification achieved by passing an examination administered by the Electronic Medical Billing Network of America, Inc.

Certified Procedural Coder (CPC): Certification achieved by passing an examination administered by the American Academy of Procedural Coders.

Charge Slip: A form the doctor fills out once you have been treated so they can send the claim to the insurance company to be paid.

Claim: A bill sent to an insurance provider, or carrier.

Claims Scrubber: Software designed to scrutinize outgoing claims before submission to clearinghouse or carrier; designed to reduce noncompliant coding errors and claim rejections.

Clean Claim: A claim that has no errors.

Clearinghouse: A program that transmits insurance claims electronically to carriers.

Comprehensive Plan: A commercial insurance plan that combines major and basic coverage.

Coordination of Benefits: A provision stating that when a patient is covered by more than one insurance plan, benefits paid by all policies are limited to 100 percent of the charges.

Co-Insurance: A percentage of the bill that must be paid by the patient; the carrier agrees to pay the rest of the bill.

Co-Payment: A payment that must be made before a doctor will see a patient (as stipulated by the insurance carrier).

Competitive Medical Plan: Permission granted by the federal government that enables an organization to write a Medicare risk contract.

Cost Contract: A contract between a Medicare program and an HMO; states that the HMO's Medicare patients will be cared for by physicians in that HMO.

Cost Plan: This is when a managed care plan allows patients to go to outside providers, and Medicare will pay its portion of the cost.

Crossover Contracts: A Medigap contract that automatically forwards Medicare claims to the Medigap insurance carrier.

Crossover Patients: Patients who have both Medicare and Medicaid coverage.

Current Procedural Terminology (CPT): A system of coding procedures, supplies, and services developed by the American Medical Association.

Customary Fee: Fee determined by insurers, based on 90 percent of fees charged by all doctors of the same specialty in the same region or geographic location.

D

Day Sheet: Used by the health care provider to list all services provided that day (used instead of one super bill per patient).

Deductible: A fee that must be paid before insurance coverage begins.

Dependent: Anyone else (spouse, child) for whom the insured is legally responsible.

Dermatology: A physician who specializes in skin and diseases of the skin.

Drop Claim to Paper: When a clearinghouse prints and mails a claim that it has received electronically.

Dual Coverage: When a patient is covered by two or more insurance policies.

Durable Medical Equipment: Medical equipment (such as a walker, hospital bed, or wheelchair) that is used within the home for any medical reason.

E

E-Codes: Classification of ICD-10-CM coding for external causes of injury; also for adverse reactions to medications.

Elective Procedure: An optional procedure that does not need to be addressed right away.

Electronic Claim: Insurance claim submitted by computer, fax, or software program.

Electronic Claims Professional (ECP): One who converts insurance claims to the standardized format and transmits them.

Electronic Claims Submission: Insurance claims that are submitted electronically by computer to the insurance company.

Electronic Medical Billing Network of America, Inc.: An association of home-based electronic medical billers.

Employer Identification Number (EIN): An EIN is used to identify a business entity; it can be obtained free from the IRS and is also known as a federal tax identification number.

Employer Group Health Plan: Private employment-based health plan that covers those who also have Medicare coverage due to their age (65 or over).

Error Report: A report sent by a clearinghouse to notify a biller of a rejected claim.

Exclusive Provider Organization (EPO): A managed care organization.

Excluded Services (or Exclusions): Services not covered by a patient's insurance policy.

Explanation of Benefits (EOB): An explanation of services provided to a person under his/her insurance policy.

Explanation of Medicare Benefits: An explanation of services provided to patients and physicians.

F

Fee-For-Service: When a physician is paid for each service performed.

Fee Schedule: A list of set fees for medical services and procedures.

Fiscal Agent: A company that processes claims for services covered under Medicare Part B and Medicaid.

Fiscal Intermediary: A company that processes claims for services covered by claims under Medicare Part A (hospitals, intermediate care facilities, home health agencies, and nursing facilities).

Full-Practice Management: Offering all services related to a physician's accounting as opposed to processing claims only.

H

Health Maintenance Organization (HMO): A managed care program that provides benefits to members who obtain services from certain health care providers; insured parties will not receive benefits if they obtain services outside their HMO network without permission; members pay a monthly fee for services.

Health Care Provider: A physician or organization that provides mental or physical health care services.

Health Information Management (HIM): HIM professionals are responsible for the creation, development, and administration of health care data reporting and collection systems that secure the integrity, quality, preservation, and availability of data for privacy, patient safety, security, and confidentiality reasons.

HIPAA: Health Insurance Portability and Accountability Act of 1996: Federal protection for personal health care records; designed to protect patient privacy.

I

ICD-10 Codes: *The International Classification of Diseases, Tenth Revision, Clinical Modification (CM)*; a coding system for medical diagnoses and procedures.

Indemnify: Reimburse health care expenses.

Indemnity Policy: An insurance policy that reimburses patients for services up to a set dollar amount.

Individual Policy: An insurance policy that has been purchased for an individual or an individual and his or her family.

Insured: The person who is covered by the insurance policy.

Intermediaries: Commercial carriers for Medicare claims.

L

Lifetime Maximum: The total amount the insurance company will pay in a lifetime for a particular problem or condition.

Limiting Charge: The amount that health care providers who do not accept Medicare can charge over and above the amount approved by Medicare.

M

Major Medical Plan: A commercial insurance plan for a major accident or illness; features large deductible and high co-payments.

Medicaid: Medical insurance coverage provided by Centers for Medicare and Medicaid Services (CMS) for those at or below poverty level.

Medicare: Medical insurance coverage for those ages 65 or over, those on social security disability, and for younger people with end-stage renal disease.

N

National Provider Identifier (NPI): The NPI is a ten-digit identification number mandated by HIPAA for health care providers. NPIs do not carry other information about health care providers, such as the state in which they live or their medical specialty. NPIs must be used in HIPAA standards transactions.

Neurology: Medical specialty that deals with diseases of the nervous system.

O

Oncology: Medical specialty that deals with tumors and cancer.

Outsourced Billing Service: Billing service that works outside of a health care provider's office.

P

Participating Physician: A physician who accepts Medicare.

Podiatry: Medical specialty that treats disorders of the foot.

Precertification: When a medical provider must obtain permission from the insurance company (the carrier) before a service can be performed on a patient.

Pre-existing Condition: A medical condition that is already present at the time an insurance policy is purchased.

R

Reasonable Fee: Fee rate billed by the doctor (one that insurers have pre-approved).

S

Self-Insured Plan: Employers (instead of insurance companies) who pay for employees' claims.

Superbill: Lists all procedures and services performed by a doctor; also contains the patient's name, charges, and the date of the visit.

T

TRICARE (formerly CHAMPUS): A government-sponsored program that provides medical services for families of active and retired military personnel and their survivors.

U

Usual, Customary, and Reasonable (UCR): Method by which insurers pay providers the usual fee, the customary fee, or the reasonable fee; method of regulating costs.

Underwriter: An insurance company that writes a policy and thus assumes liability for it.

Urology: Medical specialty that treats disorders of the urinary tract and genital tract.

W

Workers' Compensation: Private medical insurance coverage for workers who become sick or injured while working.

Bibliography

"Accounting Software Reviews." **http://accounting-software-review.toptenreviews.com**, accessed 6/1/09.

All Business. "Formatting the Financial Plan Section of a Business Plan," **www.allbusiness.com/business-planning-structures/business-plans/2527-1.html**, accessed 6/01/09.

"Assessing Clients' Needs." **http://quantum.dialog.com/media/pdfs/analyze.pdf,** accessed 6/1/09.

Burges, Marilyn, Donya Johnson, and Jim Keogh. *Medical Billing and Coding Demystified: A Self-Teaching Guide*, New York: McGraw-Hill Professional, 2006.

Bureau of Labor Statistics. **www.bls.gov/oco/ocos103.htm,** accessed 12/22/09.

Center for Medicare and Medicaid Services. **www.cms.hhs.gov/home/medicare.asp**.

Corporate Division. **www.sec.state.ma.us/cor/corpweb/corlp/lpinf.htm#VIIIf**, accessed 6/9/2009.

Coslick, Merlin B. *Medical Billing Marketing Success: Finding Local Clients, Second Edition Revised.* New Jersey: Electronic Medical Billing Network, 2001.

Coslick, Merlin B. *Medical Billing Secrets: Building Your Successful Home-Based Business.* New Jersey: Electronic Medical Billing Network of America, Inc., 2001.

Coslick, Merlin B. *Setting Up Your Medical Billing Business: Step-by-step procedures for stating and managing a computer-based electronic medical billing business.* New Jersey: Electronic Medical Billing Network,1999.

EBay. **http://pages.ebay.com/usps/shippingitems/labels.html**, accessed 6/1/2009.

EHow. "How to Ace a Business Audit," **www.ehow.com/how_2246383_ ace-business-audit.html?ref=fuel&utm_source=yahoo&utm_ medium=ssp&utm_campaign=yssp_art**, accessed 6/1/09.

Electronic Medical Billing Network. **www.medicalbillingnetwork.com/ settingupbook.htm,** accessed 12/22/09.

Endicia. **www.endicia.com/default.cfm**, accessed 6/1/2009.

Entrepreneur Press and Jennifer Dorsey. *Start Your Own Medical Claims Billing Service: Your Step-By-Step Guide to Success, 2nd Edition.* Canada: Entrepreneur Media, Inc., 2008.

Farhat, Kyle, and Nancie Cummins. *Claim Success!* Tuscon, Ariz.: Wheatmark, Inc., 2008.

Fleischner, Michael. "10 Key Components of a Marketing Plan," **www. businessknowhow.com/marketing/marketing-plan.htm**, accessed 12/22/09.

Florida Kid Care. **www.floridakidcare.org,** accessed 12/22/09.

International Revenue Service. **www.irs.gov/businesses/small/ article/0,,id=99336,00.html**, accessed 6/1/09.

Medical Coding.Net. **www.medical-coding.net/software**, accessed 6/10/2009.

Military.com. **www.military.com/benefits/tricare,** accessed 12/22/09.

MPM Soft. **www.mpmsoft.com/EDI/clearinghouse.htm**, accessed 6/07/09.

Pitney Bowes, Inc. **www.pitneyworks.com**, accessed 6/1/09.

PMIC. **http://pmiconline.stores.yahoo.net/thpapadi20.html**, accessed 12/22/09.

The Practice of Medical Billing and Coding: A Real Life Book, Second Edition, New Jersey: ICDC Publishing, Inc., 2006.

Rimmer, Michelle M. *Medical Billing 101*, Delmar, Cengage Learning, 2007.

Scott, Alice, and Michele Redmond. *The Basics of Medical Billing*, Solutions Medical Billing, Inc., 2008.

Stamps.com. **www.stamps.com/welcome/custom/home01/index1. html**, accessed 6/1/2009.

U.S. Patent and Trademark Office: Trademark FAQ. **www.uspto.gov/ web/offices/tac/tmfaq.htm#Basic**, accessed 6/9/2009.

U.S. Postal Service. **https://sss-web.usps.com/cns/landing.do**, accessed 6/3/2009.

U.S. Department of Labor. **www.dol.gov/owcp**, accessed 12/22/09.

Ward, Susan. "Writing the Business Plan Section 8," **http://sbinfo-canada.about.com/cs/businessplans/a/bizplanfinanc.htm**, accessed 6/2/09.

Web Office. **www.villagemall.com.au/content/smallbus/profit_planning.htm**, accessed 6/1/09.

Yalden, Claudia A. *Medical Billing, The Bottom Line, An Entrepreneur's Guide*, Morris Publishing Company, 2007.

Author Biography

Laura Gater is a freelance writer based in northeast Indiana. She has written thousands of medical, health care, business, and travel articles for both trade and consumer publications. When she is not writing, she enjoys the outdoors, reading, her family, and pets. She has written *Writing for Professional Medical Publications* (**www.booklocker.com/books/999. html**), *Small Practice Survival Guide* (Doctor's Digest), and *Your Practice and the Recession* (Doctor's Digest).

Index